WITHDRAWN

# Sholem Aleichem in the Theater

## Jacob Weitzner

**JEWS IN MODERN CULTURE
SYMPOSIUM PRESS**

Madison • Teaneck

**Fairleigh Dickinson University Press**

Associated University Presses
440 Forsgate Drive
Cranbury, NJ 08512

*Library of Congress Cataloging-in-Publication Data*

Weitzner, Jacob
   Sholem Aleichem in the theater / by Jacob Weitzner.
     p. cm. – (Jews in Modern Culture)
   Includes bibliographical references and index.
   1. Sholem Aleichem, 1859-1916 – Stage history. 2. Sholem Aleichem, 1859-1916 – Dramatic works. I. Title. II. Series.
PJ5129.R2Z885 1994
792.9'5 – dc20                                      94-5295
                                                                             CIP

© *1994 by Science Reviews, Northwood*

*All rights reserved. Authorization to photocopy items for internal or personal use, or the internal or personal use of specific clients, is granted by the copyright owner, provided that a base fee of $10.00, plus eight cents per page, per copy is paid directly to the Copyright Clearance Center, 222 Rosewood Drive, Danvers, Massachusetts 01923. [0-8386-3636-5/94 $10.00 + 8¢ pp, pc.]*

*Printed in Great Britain by Lonsdale Press Ltd, London*

# About the Author

Dr. Jacob (Kobi) Weitzner is an authority on Jewish theater in both Yiddish and Hebrew. He translated with Dr. Barnett Zumoff, *The Jackpot,* and their's is the only translation of a full length Sholem Aleichem play in English.

He currently teaches Yiddish literature at the Open University and Hebrew literature at the Tel Aviv University's overseas program.

The author is the only internationally recognized contemporary Yiddish playwright. Eli Wallach in The New York Times hailed his play *Karpilevski Or What Is To Be Done With Him* as "a well written, witty play with philosophical and political overtones".

Dr. Weitzner is currently working on a book about the biblical story of the selling of Joseph in the Jewish folk theater – the *Purimshpil.*

# Sholem Aleichem in the Theater

## Contents

| | |
|---|---|
| 1. The life of Sholem Aleichem | 1 |
| 2. From page to stage: The problems in the realization of written text on stage. | 8 |
| 3. Stempenyu | 12 |
| 4. The Treasure | 39 |
| 5. Tevye the Dairyman | 74 |
| 6. The Jackpot | 111 |
| 7. Epilogue | 150 |
| Notes | 153 |
| Selected Bibliography of the Plays | 173 |
| Index | 179 |

# 1. The Life of Sholem Aleichem

Sholem Aleichem, (Shalom Rabinovitz) the greatest and the most popular Yiddish writer, was born in 1859 in Pereyaslav, Ukraine. He was educated in a Kheyder - a traditional Jewish primary school. His father, a grain and lumber merchant, failed in business and the family became poor. His mother died of cholera when Sholem was thirteen. His father remarried. Sholem Aleichem wrote in his autobiography From The Fair [Funem yarid]*[1]* that his first literary work was a dictionary of his stepmother's curses. His father was religious, but valued secular education. He did not send him to continue his studies at a yeshiva, a talmudic academy. Instead young Sholem was sent to a Russian high school where he finished with distinction. After graduation he was hired by Elimelech Loyev, a wealthy Jewish landowner, as a private tutor for his daughter, Olga. A new world opened for him. Life on Loyev's estate was luxurious. Dinner was served by domestics in uniform. The tutor and his student spent their free time together. A favorite pastime was horse back riding in the woods owned by the family. Sholem Aleichem was seventeen, his student was fourteen, and they fell in love. Loyev was furious when he found out about his daughter's secret love. Sholem Aleichem was fired. He found a position as a government Rabbi in the town of Lubny. Government Rabbis were not considered by the Jewish community to be their religious leaders, but rather tolerated as government officials they had to put up with. Nevertheless, these positions enabled educated young Jews like Sholem Aleichem to make a living. The young lovers kept in contact and married against

Olga's father's wishes in 1883. Sholem Aleichem was twenty-four, Olga was twenty-one. Eventually Loyev reconciled with the young couple. He demanded though that Sholem Aleichem quit his not quite respectable job as a government Rabbi. Elimelech Loyev died in 1885. At the age of twenty-six Sholem Aleichem became the man in charge of the large Loyev estate. The young couple moved to Kiev in 1887, where they lived until 1890. The years between his marriage at the age of twenty-four and his departure from Kiev at the age of twenty-nine were the happiest years in Sholem Aleichem's life. These were also his formative years as a writer.

Like most young aspiring Jewish writers in Eastern Europe at the time, Sholem Aleichem started writing in Hebrew. Yiddish was regarded as an inferior idiom of expression. The literary language was Hebrew - the language of the Bible. Jewish writers used Hebrew even when they portrayed Yiddish speaking characters. Sholem Aleichem was a great communicator, and it was only natural for him to pick Yiddish, the language of the masses. His desire to be closer to his readership made him also adopt the pen name of "Sholem Aleichem" ["Peace be with you"], a common greeting among Yiddish speaking Jews, a kind of "How do you do". Sholem Rabinowitz picked a popular Yiddish expression as his pen name, not unlike his contemporary Samuel Langhorne Clemens who chose a Mississippi sailors' expression as his *nom de plume:* Mark Twain. Sholem Aleichem wrote feuilletons, stories, one act plays, and novellas. *The Pocket Knife [Dos Messerl],* published in 1887, received a favorable critique from the Jewish Russian historian Shimon Dubnov, and encouraged Sholem Aleichem to pursue a career as a writer. In the years 1888 and 1889 Sholem Aleichem published at his expense The Jewish Folk Library [Di Yidishe Folksbibliotek] [2] a first of its kind Yiddish literary anthology. Sholem Aleichem was then a young millionaire, and the handsome sums he paid out of his own pocket encouraged writers who until then wrote only in Hebrew, to turn to Yiddish. I. L. Peretz published his poem *Monish*, and Mendele Moykher Sforim (Abramowitz) renewed his writing in Yiddish with an extended version of his *Wish-Ring [Vintshfingerl]* for Sholem Aleichem's Jewish Folk Library. Sholem Aleichem introduced to the

Jewish public more than new Jewish writers. He introduced a whole new literature. The Jewish Folk Library legitimized Yiddish as a worthy entrant to world literature. It was an eye opener to many young Jews. It showed them that they could write modern, sophisticated literature, not only in the respective languages of their countries or in Hebrew, but in the language they actually spoke: Yiddish. Thus Sholem Aleichem was not only the greatest writer modern Yiddish Literature had, but also its greatest promoter. Sholem Aleichem published two of his own novellas in the *Yidishe Folksbibliotek*: *Stempenyu* and *Yosele Nightingale [Yosele Solovey]*. *Stempenyu* was the story of a fiddler and his unhappy love affair with a married woman. Sholem Aleichem later adapted the novella for the theater when he first arrived in New York in 1907. In 1890, at the age of thirty-one, Sholem Aleichem lost his fortune, or rather his wife's fortune, on the Kiev stock exchange. Sholem Aleichem who just a few years before was a wealthy patron of needy Yiddish writers, suddenly became one. The years that followed his bankruptcy were poor in literary output, yet he never stopped writing. In 1894 he wrote *YOKENHOZ Or The Big Stock Exchange Game [YOKENOZ oder Dos Groyse Berzenshpil]*[3]. His famed "Never do well" character Menachem Mendel who was in all likelihood inspired by his painful personal experience in the stock exchange, figured in the play. This was Sholem Aleichem's first attempt at a full length play. The play lacked coherence but the characters' portrayals were excellent. People in the Jewish community thought the comedy portrayed them unfavorably. They lobbied with the authorities and the publication of the play was banned. In the same year, 1894, Sholem Aleichem wrote his first Tevye monologues: *Unworthy me [Katonti]*, and *The Jackpot [Dos Groyse Gevins]*. Interestingly, Tevye the dairyman, the famed patriarchal figure of Yiddish literature was created by a young man of thirty-five. Theater at this point in Sholem Aleichem's life was only a marginal activity. The ban on Yiddish theater in the Russian empire was lifted only in 1908, and Sholem Aleichem was not yet acquainted with the American Yiddish theater. Sholem Aleichem relied mostly on the fast expanding Yiddish press to publish his work. Newspapers, aside from being a source of information, provided literary entertainment. They published stories and serial novels by popular writers - the equivalent of today's television series. Thanks to his continuous literary contribution to the popular press, Sholem Aleichem's popularity rose steadily and he became the most well known and beloved Jewish writer.

In 1903 he wrote another drama: *Scattered and dispersed [Tseseyt un tseshpreyt].*[5] The play portrayed the crisis of a Jewish family in a changing world. The same theme, placed in a different setting, was treated later in his best drama: *Tevye The Dairyman [Tevye Der Milkhiker]*. The play premiered in the "Elyseum" theater in Warsaw in 1905. Warsaw was then part of the Russian empire and the play could not be performed in the original because of the ban on Yiddish theater. In spite of its many shortcomings the play received an enthusiastic reception from the Jewish public. The popular success of the play encouraged Sholem Aleichem to pursue a career in the theater. In a letter to his daughter he wrote:

"What shall I tell you about yesterday's triumph? I used to take part in ovations to beloved artists, but I never saw anything of the likes of yesterday, not even in my artistic fantasy. After the first act I was (literally) covered with flowers. Then, at the end of each act, I was called to the stage. During the fourth act, the public simply lost its self-control, and cheered every sentence that had any relation to the theme of the play. When the curtain fell hats started flying, and a kind of raw force was about to swallow me. For a while I was afraid the theater would collapse, and was weary of demonstrations. I cannot explain this phenomenon: is the popularity of the folk writer so huge, or is it because the people are starved for a Jewish theater, or maybe the mob is savage by nature? At the exit, a mob of thousands was ambushing his victim. Thanks to the wise advise of the police, I was locked up in a balcony for half an hour, and then got out of the theater through a back door. God almighty, can you imagine what would have happened if we could perform in Yiddish? My fate and your future (I make here an appeal to my successors) are closely tied to the Jewish theater. Write it down in your diary. In the meantime I kiss you dearest. Oh, how much I wanted to be present on your birthday.

Will it be possible? I don't know, because I am short of money. As of now others harvest the fruits of my labor, not me."[7]

From that period on the theater became an important part of Sholem Aleichem's work. He made an unsuccessful attempt to found an artistic Yiddish theater in Odessa. In the same year, 1905, shattered by the pogrom in Kiev, Sholem Aleichem and his family left Russia. Geneva, Switzerland, served them, as it did many Russian exiles, as a temporary harbor.

In 1907 Sholem Aleichem came to New York for the first time. New York at the turn of the century was the center of Yiddish theater. The masses of recent Jewish immigrants looked for a place where they could feel at home, and the Yiddish theater was that place.

The two rival stars of the Yiddish stage, Adler and Thomashefski, wanted Sholem Aleichem to write for their theaters. Sholem Aleichem made the mistake of accepting both offers. I. D. Berkowitz, Sholem Aleichem's son-in-law and literary collaborator, wrote about the circumstances that pushed Sholem Aleichem to this double deal:

"His situation got him trapped with writing simultaneously two comedies for two theaters. Adler whom he appreciated most as an actor forced him into that situation. Adler was however very difficult when it came to money...Thomashefsky, unlike Adler behaved as a gentleman and offered Sholem Aleichem a thousand dollars in cash for his play...Dire need forced Sholem Aleichem to accept the quite impossible task of writing two theater plays at the same time."[8]

February 8, 1907 was the opening night for two Sholem Aleichem plays. Boris Thomashefsky's People's Theater premiered with *Jewish Daughters - or - Stempenyu [Yidishe Tekhter - oder -Stempenyu]*,[9] and Jacob Adler's "Grand Theater" premiered with *The Scum - or - Shmuel Pasternak [Der Oysvurf - oder - Shmuel Pasternak]*, an adaption of his first full length comedy "YOKENHOZ".

Both Thomashefski and Adler were angry at him because they did not get what they wanted, namely the only Sholem Aleichem play in town. There was only one thing that could have appeased them—success at the box office. Unfortunately the two hastily written plays were artistic and financial failures. What was supposed to be the start of a promising career with the New York Yiddish theater was finished before it began. Sholem Aleichem returned to his family in Geneva. In spite of these disappointments and bad health, Sholem Aleichem continued writing. In 1907 he rewrote his Tevye monologues as a theater play. He sent *Tevye* to the stars of the Yiddish theater in New York but after the commercial failure of his former plays, they refused to be associated with him. His bad plays ruined the chances of his good ones.

The history of world theater offers many examples of playwrights who took a long time to find their voice in the theater. Molière wrote bad tragedies for twenty years before he wrote his great comedies but unlike Sholem Aleichem he did not depend on anybody for a break. He had his own theater. Sholem Aleichem depended on the capricious stars of the Yiddish theater to produce his plays.

In 1908 he wrote a new comedy: *The Treasure [Der Oytser]*[10] which suffered the same fate as *Tevye*; the stars of the Yiddish theater would not touch it.

From his base in Geneva Sholem Aleichem went on lecture tours in the Jewish centers of Eastern Europe. He read from his works to enthusiastic crowds who came to see and hear their beloved folk writer. In the summer of 1908, during one of these tours, he fell ill with severe tuberculosis. He was then forty-nine.

In 1909, his fiftieth birthday was celebrated throughout the Jewish world. A committee was set up with the specific purpose of acquiring the rights to his books from the publishers and giving them back to the ailing writer.

The following seven years Sholem Aleichem was assured a steady income from his publications and enjoyed relative security. The outbreak of the First World War plunged Europe into turmoil. His situation became desperate. The income from the sale of his books in Europe had stopped. The income from the Eastern European Yiddish newspapers was lost. In spite of unpleasant past experience, Sholem Aleichem and his family emigrated to New York. In the brief American chapter in Sholem Aleichem's life that lasted from 1914 until his untimely death at the age of 57 in 1916, Sholem Aleichem wrote his best comedy *The Jackpot [Dos Groyse Gevins]*[11] which too, was rejected by the Yiddish theater. Ten years later, New York would have artistic Yiddish theaters such as Maurice Schwartz's "Der Yidisher Kunst Teater" or the "Artef". But in 1915 the business of the Yiddish theater was business. The people who ran it were not sure about Sholem Aleichem's artistic merit, but they remembered well his box office failures. They were determined not to lose money on a Sholem Aleichem play again. In the last years Sholem Aleichem started writing his biography From the Fair [Funem Yarid], which he did not live to finish. His son Misha who stayed in Europe died in the summer of 1915. The death of his son shattered the ailing writer. For the first time in his life he lost his optimism. He died the following year, on May 13th, 1916. The people of New York who turned a cold shoulder to the writer when he needed help most, came in the hundreds of thousands to his funeral. It was the largest funeral procession New York ever saw.

## 2. From Page to Stage: The problems in the realization of written text on stage

Drama is written to be performed. This book concerns itself not only with the genesis of Sholem Aleichem's plays in the writer's workshop, but also with their various productions in the theater. Most people see, not read plays. A play to them is not only the written text, but also the way it is presented on stage. This is perhaps the reason why we do not consider unperformed plays as genuine dramatic works. Playwrights feel the same way, and this explains the desperate efforts Sholem Aleichem made to get his plays produced.

Theater is a combination of text and its performance on stage. Most people will agree with that. The problem starts when one tries to define the relationship between the text and its performance. To Berkowitz, who adapted *The Treasure* for the Hebrew national theater Habima, the text was everything. He warned the actors not to drop an iota of his dramatic adaptation. Plays however, are never produced exactly as written. Sholem Aleichem knew it and was less protective of his work than his adaptor. Sholem Aleichem and Berkowitz embraced two different approaches to the theater. Berkowitz represented the textual approach. The textual approach demands of the performance to be a faithful rendition of the text. Sholem Aleichem took a more theatrical approach, one that granted the performance a life of its own.

The textual approach argues that the text is the main thing, and the performance is only its reproduction on stage. Partisans of that approach can refer to Aristotle[1] who claimed that the power of drama comes out in the reading, and the performance is at best, secondary. The partisans of the textual approach are for the most part less extreme than Aristotle. They do want to see the text performed, but with as little changes as possible. To them a good director is one that takes the text and puts it on stage as is. This sounds simple, but it is not as simple as it sounds. One cannot simply relocate a text from the page to the stage. The performance is not the same thing as the text only in a different setting, but rather something else altogether. We can go to the bank and exchange Dollars for English pounds, because Dollars and Pounds are the same thing, that is money, only in two variations (American and English currencies). $ and £ are both signs of the same language, the language of finances. In the theater however, the transition from text to performance requires a transition from one system of signs, the written language, to a different system of signs, the stage language, which is made out of the spoken word, movement, lighting, acting, music and scenery. The play and the play on stage are not the same thing only in different forms.

Topol portrayed an exuberant Tevye on stage, Maurice Schwartz portrayed a philosophical one. In the transition from page to stage the play wins some or loses some. One thing is certain. It never remains the same. The change in form inexorably brings about a change in substance.

Like any literary text, the dramatic text has within it a set of gaps. Each and every director fills the many gaps in the text as he pleases. In the scene where Hava is about to marry her Christian lover Fedya, many questions remain unanswered by Sholem Aleichem. We know that Hava is brokenhearted over the break up with her family, and that Fedya tells her not to be sad. We do not know however if he pleads with her passionately, or angrily. Is he holding her, or moving away from her? If he is holding her, is he holding her tenderly, or in a way that suggests sexual desire? Those are but a few examples of the gaps in the dramatic text. The director has to fill these gaps with audio visual signs. The way in which a director uses the actors, the musicians, the stage designers is very personal. For that reason we cannot speak of text and its performance as identical, interchangeable entities.

The partisans of the textual approach concede that the text can be performed in various ways, but they staunchly maintain that there is in fact only one good performance of a given text.

The danger in this argument is that this chosen performance, which supposedly interprets the text best, suffocates the creative pleasure of reading and directing plays. The director ceases to be a creative artist. His job narrows down to making reproductions of that ideal performance. That ideal performance is often a previous performance that the critics liked. Paradoxically, the insistence on an authentic rendition of the play, sanctifies less the text, and more a specific interpretation of it. The partisans of the textual approach end up making a fetish of one historical performance.

The textual approach to the theater has therefor its problems. The opposite approach, the theatrical one, is not without problems either. The theatrical approach which in many cases becomes anti-textual, refuses to accept the text as a substantial ingredient of the performance. The theater, plead the partisans of this school, is only the process which takes place in front of the audience. The text, in as much as it exists, is only one of the ingredients of the performance, and not necessarily the most important one. The major problem with this argument is that the anti-textualists define themselves by the very thing they oppose: The text. They modify it, they give it new interpretations, they put it in a different historical context. There seems to be one thing they chose not to do with the text: To do without it. The part the text plays in a non-textual theater brings to mind a conversation that took place between the director Granovsky and the theater historian Zylbercweig. Zylbercweig wrote it down in his *Lexicon of the Yiddish Theater*:

"I once asked Granovsky after a performance of 200 000 (*The Jackpot*) by Sholem Aleichem:
- How many of the Sholem Aleichem original lines are left in your version of the play?
- Give or take forty lines - he answered very seriously.

- I doubt if there are even forty lines left from the Sholem Aleichem original - I said.
- Maybe not. It doesn't matter though. Sholem Aleichem did not write for our theater, and we are not in the business of reconstructing the original Sholem Aleichem text in the theater. What we want is to uncover the internal substance of Sholem Aleichem's work, a substance that still touches us today".[2]

Granovsky probably used more than forty lines of Sholem Aleichem's text, but even if he used as little as forty lines, he illustrated thereby the paradox of the non-textual director. He felt free to do with the text as he pleased. He was, however, not text free.

The director is thus caught between the text and the performance. In fact he lives off the perpetual conflict between the two. He plays the arbitrator. In the process he creates a new text, a stage text. When Koltun, in Rotboym's version of *The Jackpot*, says that lottery tickets never win, he bangs his cane on the floor, pushes his belly forward, and puffs up his cheeks. The sum of his movements, speech intonations and pauses, create a second text, one that runs parallel to the original text. Alongside the text of the playwright surges a secondary text, that of the director.

The theatrical text continues to represent a problem even after it is no longer under the double authority of the playwright and the director. Sometimes the text receives a new significance, given to it not by the theater, but by a historical situation. Tevye's struggle to survive takes on another dimension after the Holocaust. Here the importance of the director emerges again. He is the person who has to take a stand regarding the text. Is he going to emphasize the national tragedy or the personal tragedy of Tevye?

The theater, this blend of text and its performances, is apparently sentenced to perpetual renewal. In this book we shall deal with the historic continuity of the performances of four major plays by Sholem Aleichem. We will follow each play from its genesis in the workshop of Sholem Aleichem through the modifications of the directors, to the final stamp given to it by the actors. A question that we will keep in mind is whether we can perceive a historical development in the performance of Sholem Aleichem's work in the Jewish theater.

# 3. Stempenyu

Sholem Aleichem saw in shund literature, the popular Yiddish literature, in which cheap romanticism was mingled with sensational, unrealistic plots, an evil which had to be uprooted. *Stempenyu* was meant to serve as an antithesis to the shund literature. In 1888 Sholem Aleichem published *The Trial of Shomer [Shomer's Mishpet]*.[1] In the book he put the sensational novelist Nokhem Meyer Sheikevitch, known as Shomer, on trial. After he humorously exposed the literary and moral shortcomings in Sheikevitch's novels, Sholem Aleichem showed a positive example in his novel *Stempenyu*.[2] Thus, *Stempenyu* was supposed to be more than just another book. It was meant to be the pioneer of a new literary genre: The Jewish Novel. In fact the novel published in the Jewish Folk library in 1888, had a secondary title: "A Jewish Novel." In its preface, written in the form of a letter to "grandfather" Mendele Moykher Sforim, the young (31) Sholem Aleichem explained the meaning of the term: "Jewish Novel." Sholem Aleichem fully agreed with Mendele that love in the Jewish community was completely different from love in the gentile world. Hence the mimesis of the romantic life in the Jewish community, the Jewish novel, had to be different from that of the European novel. The central point of the Jewish novel was the willingness of the characters to put moral obligation over love. In Stempenyu as in many European novels, the love is a forbidden one, but in the "Jewish Novel" of Sholem Aleichem, the married woman, albeit afflicted and tormented, does not betray her husband, and ultimately finds love within the marriage.

## The Attempt to Open a Second Front Against Shund

*Stempenyu*, the Jewish novel, was part of Sholem Aleichem's war against the shund literature.

By means of the dramatic adaptation of the novel, Sholem Aleichem wanted to open another front against shund, this time in the theater. Unknowingly Sholem Aleichem followed Wolfson's footsteps. Both Wolfson and Sholem Aleichem not only went against a theatrical phenomenon they thought harmful, but also created dramatic material to substitute for it. Wolfson wrote Frivolity and Hypocrisy [*Leichtsin und Fromelei*][3] with the declared intent to provide a dramatic substitute with literary value to what he considered to be a shameful social and theatrical phenomenon, that is the Jewish folk theater, the "Purimshpil." A hundred years later Sholem Aleichem came out with a similar effort to change the face of the Jewish theater. In 1905 three factors impelled Sholem Aleichem to undertake a significant creative work for the Jewish theater. In the beginning of the same year, the Czar's interdiction against Yiddish theater was abolished. In April 1905 Sholem Aleichem was present at the performance of his play, *Scattered and Dispersed*, which was done in Polish in the Elyseum Theater in Warsaw. The play was a huge success. At the same time Sholem Aleichem and Spivakovsky came to an agreement, by which Sholem Aleichem would be the playwright at residence and artistic director of Spivakosky's theater. Encouraged by all these things, Sholem Aleichem addressed his fellow writers. Instead of deriding the Yiddish theater, he called upon them to improve it. In the newspaper Der Veg he wrote:

"Instead of sharpening our tongues, and being wise guys, pointing out others' errors, writing long critiques and papers on art, we would be better off beginning to work on writing plays, plays! Our task is to create a repertoire, a tiny repertoire, a young one, maybe not a ripe one, but at least some repertoire. Let's give something to the theater of our people! Let the actors not argue like the Jews in Egypt; straw is not given us, we don't get any material, and bricks they tell us, you should make..."[4]

## *Stempenyu* - the Play

Sholem Aleichem put himself to work. *Stempenyu* was meant to be the first in a line of quality plays, which would begin a new era for the Yiddish theater.

It seemed as if the theater people themselves were ready for a change. In a letter to Sholem Aleichem, Thomashefsky, the star and owner of the People's Theater complained about the low level of the Yiddish theater in New York. Thomashefsky promised Sholem Aleichem that his theater, the People's Theater, was making an effort to present plays of merit:

"The other playwrights, like Lateiner, Hurwitz, Zeifert, Shaikevitch, Rakov, Katz, Miller, Yakebter, Zalatrowski, Bilder and many more shund writers, produce historical and family dramas overnight. In other words they take a German or an English play, and make Jews out of the Gentiles. Katharine becomes Sheindl, Count So and So becomes Rabbi Abraham Ashkenazi, or another nice sounding name of a respectable Jew. They throw in a little music, nice songs, beautiful scenery, and the play is ready to go. The simple folk loves those things, and pays to see them. The more refined spectators however want better plays. We search for better plays. We are also glad to pay for them, provided we can get them. Our theater, 'The Peoples Theater' is a literary one. That is we aspire to perform better plays, and we do so as much as we can."[5]

The stars of the Yiddish theater paid lip service to art, but in reality they were interested first and foremost in box office success. They thought that Sholem Aleichem had to spice up his plays to make them more commercial. Sholem Aleichem had to change the text to please their taste and deliver a melodramatic version of the play that ended with the heroine's suicide. He had to surrender because as he said: "What can you do when America gives orders." In a letter to an American friend he wrote:

"My Dear Friend, Dr. Fishberg. Kiev Hotel Imperial, October 25, 1905.

I send you the fifth act of 'Stempenyu'. A new act, instead of the former one. With a death, as America demands. A Jewish heroine, in my opinion, seldom poisons herself for the sake of love. But what can you do when America gives an order? Show the fifth act to Mr. Adler. He should have a good look at the entire play. He should perform it once with all the details - and he'll see what I am capable of. No more now. I'm sick. Our life here is worth a penny."[6]

In the end it was Thomashefsky, not Adler who performed the play.

In 1907 the People's Theater of Boris Thomashefsky presented *Stempenyu or Jewish Daughters - a Drama in 4 Acts* by Sholem Aleichem. The play was never published. A copy of the manuscript is kept in the YIVO Archive in New York.[7]

## The Transformation

A general change in the work is noticeable when one compares the play and the novel, both by Sholem Aleichem. A crude sentimentality washes over the play.

In both the novel and the play, Sholem Aleichem described the attraction young women felt for Stempenyu. In the novel the young women who fall under Stempenyu's spell are referred to in frenchified Yiddish as 'demoiselles', in a light hearted parody on shund literature.

"Let alone the girls, the demoiselles they remained standing nailed to their spots, looking at Stempenyu with his magic violin, motionless. Not a blink of the eye, but somewhere there on the other side of their corset, their heart pounds: tic, tic, and often a hidden sigh escapes."[8]

The ironical tone is all but gone in the play. Lachrymose emotionalism, as seen in the following passage, took its place:

"Etel: Stempenyu? You foolish girl, wait until you hear him after the wedding ceremony when they serve the soup!...Stempenyu, huh, how many girls and young women in your opinion have already lost their lives over him and his music?"[9]

The comic undertones of the romantic plot disappear completely in the transition from the novel to the play. The-light hearted sentimentality of the novel is replaced in the play by a heavy-handed emotionalism, the very emotionalism that Sholem Aleichem had sworn to eradicate from the Yiddish theater.

## The Depreciation of the Characters

In the transition from the novel to the play the characters lose not only wit but also psychological depth. The good become very good, the bad become very bad, and the clashes between them become obvious and therefore uninteresting.

Rachel's husband, Moyshe Menashe is an example. In the novel Moyshe Menashe was portrayed as somewhat vain and self centered. He lived his small selfish life shuttling between the synagogue, the family business and the market place, leaving his wife, Rachel, alone with her boredom. Still he had a sincere love for his wife, even though it became evident only when she fell ill. In his novel, Sholem Aleichem put the blame more on society than on Moyshe Menashe for the mediocre nature of the relationship between husband and wife. In the play Moyshe Menashe is to blame. He lost the little psychological depth he had in the novel, and was flattened out to fit the stereotype of the ludicrous *Hasid* of the Haskala (Enlightenment) plays. Moyshe Menashe became the spiritual double of Goldfaden's Kuni Leml without having his physical comic attributes. He had both the ideological narrow mindedness of the bad guy of the Haskala comedies, and the anemic persona of its good guys.

The characters in the drama are shaped by interaction. Juliet has to be seductive for Romeo to want her. In a domino like effect, one weak character generates another weak character.

The following dialogue between Moyshe Menashe and Rachel is a good example. Moyshe Menashe picks on this wife and mocks her reading the *Tsene Rene*, a popular version of the Bible, written in Yiddish especially for women:

"Menashe: Rejoice in thy reign...What chapter did you open to? Ha ha...women's Bible...Ha ha ha...

Well yes, huh!...Men...Sure...Men are men. And women are...huh...females. (Prays loud) Rejoice in thy reign, the observant of Sabbath.

Rachel: What about women? Women are not humans?...Don't we have the same heads as you. The same eyes? The same hands?"[10]

The dialogue sounds as if it were taken out of a shund play with maskilic pretensions. It rings more like an exchange of slogans than a talk. Moyshe Menashe and Rachel become walking banners. There is no symbiosis between the ideological content and the characters who are supposedly their mouthpieces.

In his novel Sholem Aleichem criticized Jewish society of the time. Sholem Aleichem was critical of the completely passive role women were forced to assume in the family and in the community. In the play Sholem Aleichem intensified the social criticism. Paradoxically the criticism rang hollower as it became fiercer. Thus Rachel responds angrily to her husband's mockery:

"Why are you laughing? Have we got any other Bible to read? You know only one thing to mock us. Why don't you see to it to give us something better to read than this bible for women? Men."[11]

For Rachel to come out with a feminist-like manifesto of this kind is hardly believable. Sholem Aleichem explained her character:

"Rachel was a simple Jewish young woman, without fancy ideals, without guile, in short - what has been called a Kosher Jewish daughter."[12]

Characters can change, but it is the business of the playwright to show us how and why. In the play Rachel simply jump-cuts from one persona to another.

## The return to Shund

Rachel's friend, Chaya Etel also lost credibility in the transition from the novel to the play. Chaya Etel gave Rachel what Flaubert would have called her sentimental education. From her she heard for the first time words like "romance" and "love". Through her she was exposed to the notion of adultery.

Chaya Etel was married off against her will to an elderly, repulsive man, withered away and died. The Chaya Etel story with all its lachrymose aspects was perhaps a plausible one in the Jewish reality of the time. Still, as Luckacz noticed "literature has to be careful even when registering absolutely authentic cases."[13] The treatment of the character in the novel is delicate, whereas the treatment in the play is heavy handed. Racked with pain, Chaya Etel coughs up blood and dies as the curtain descends on the first act.

Although Chaya Etel is dead by the end of act one, she remains a force in the play, guiding Rachel through the action. Her tragic end also prefigures the destiny that awaits Rachel. In fact she reappears as a ghost, who personifies Rachel's super ego, interferes in her forbidden love affair with Stempenyu, and attempts to make Rachel renounce this illicit union.

"Chaya Etel: Time...to light the candles...light the candles...and pray God for yourself...and for you heavy sins...

Rachel: For my great sins...

Chaya Etel: You forgot...that you are a Jewish daughter...a married woman...

Rachel: A married woman...

Chaya Etel: Almighty Father...who is blessed and feared in heaven...may his name last forever."[14]

In drama, the ghost is often given the opportunity to fulfil an intrinsic need that was denied him during his life-time, like Khonen in The Dybbuk or the most famous of all dramatic ghosts, the King of Denmark in *Hamlet*. Chaya Etel however delivers lines completely alien to her character. In life Chaya Etel was a frail, helpless woman. As a ghost she becomes quite unexpectedly, a reprimanding prophet of doom. The result is a hardly credible dramatic character. When Rachel meets Stempenyu in a lane in front of the monastery Chaya Etel's ghost sneaks up to reprove and torment her:

"Chaya Etel: Thou shall accept from your high seat the prayers of the pure souls who stand in front of your throne of honor and pray...merely for the living...who are full of crimes and sins..."[15]

Stempenyu who doesn't see the ghost goes on with his amorous confession.

"We will be happy! Famous and happy! No more Stempenyu...goodbye...Stempenyu...Paganini...Paganini...Paganini...

Rachel: Woe is me. My life is a misery. She is here."[16]

Rachel runs for her life and leaves Stempenyu in despair. What makes this scene particularly cheap, is the religious flavor which has been added to it. Sholem Aleichem has surrendered here to exigencies of the New York Yiddish theater, which gave its audience a little of everything: Pretty actresses, songs, and a pinch of Religion. The appearance of Chaya Etel as a righteous soul, who came from the dead to bring Rachel back to the right path, was an appropriate dessert for such a menu. In the commercial Yiddish theater it did not seem to matter at all if the character, here Chaya Etel, stood in complete contradiction to the text she delivered. The Jewish theater goer who shaved his beard and left the orthodox Jewish life behind when he came to America, liked to hear a fragment of "Kol Nidrey" or see the ceremony of the sabbath candles lighting. It did not matter a bit if this religious touch was irrelevant to the plot or the characters. The audience liked it therefor the playwright had to provide it. The problem with this approach was that the play lost its authenticity in the process. The charming folk song became a cheap theatrical couplet, and the religious ritual turned into a vulgar exhibition. The composer Joseph Rumshinsky wrote:

"Once at a rehearsal of Sholem Aleichem's *'Jewish Daughters'* (*Stempenyu*), Thomashefsky asked me to write down the notes of a song that Sholem Aleichem knew. Sholem Aleichem sang it for me. It was called "Oh, oh, it's called 'kugel', and it melts in your mouth." When Sholem Aleichem sang it for me in his way, I felt like asking him to sing more folk melodies of this kind. But I was too shy to do so. I thought to myself that the melody with the words - the way he sang them - had all the charm in the world, but in the theater on stage, it came out sounding like a cheap couplet. It lost all the Sholem Aleichem charm, the folksy thing. They added more words, the so-called lyrics, and Fridzl squeezed in tunes and drowned the folksy quality of Sholem Aleichem. Not only the tune, but the whole play drowned in cheap theatrical effects. After Sholem Aleichem read the text for the entire ensemble, and was applauded for his delivery, the actor, Mogulesco, said that if the actors played only fifty percent of the way Sholem Aleichem read it, the play would be the greatest success. But, he added he was afraid it would not have the hoped for success because the tone, the atmosphere of Sholem Aleichem was missing. And Mogulesco was right. It was a terrible performance."[17]

Shmuel Niger said of Sholem Aleichem that two forces fought over his literary soul.[18] Mendele was his guardian angel and Shomer his devil. Hence the criticism of Shomer echoes the private war between Sholem Aleichem and the literary virus within himself. In order to fight it more effectively Sholem Aleichem externalized it in the person of Shomer. If Shomer is Sholem Aleichem's literary id, Mendele is his super ego. In his foreword to the novel, *Stempenyu*, Sholem Aleichem invited Mendele, the purist of Yiddish literature, to lean over his shoulder and ban any incursion of literary trash:

"I know dear Grandpa, I feel it, how necessary it was to purify 'Stempenyu' in many waters. Certainly, with you, 'Stempenyu' would come out completely different. With you Grandpa we would have had here a story about a story, a story within a story, and the story itself."[19]

The war against shund in the novel was an inner struggle for the writer. Since he wrote the play, it became a confrontation between the author and the performers. The dramatic adaptation was done as part of a business deal between Sholem Aleichem and Thomashefsky, the star and owner of the People's Theater. Commercial considerations decided from that moment on the shape of the play. The demand for the addition of songs and lyrics and the tendency to use "strong effects" which would carry the audience away, brought *Stempenyu* to a level comparable to the shund theater so hated by the writer.

## *Stempenyu* in Habima

Shmuel Bunim adapted and directed the play in the Israeli National Theater, Habima, in 1972. He reused the same adaptation for the production of the Folksbine theater, in 1973 in New York.

Bunim had access to both the novel and the play as raw material for his dramatic adaptation. Bunim decided to leave out Sholem Aleichem's criticism of the shund theater in his version of the play. Sholem Aleichem's campaign against shund in the theater are not known to the public today, he argues. The general public in Israel and in America is not familiar with the Yiddish theater and its problem with shund. The older, Yiddish speaking public on the other hand, explains Bunim, is not interested in changing it. In fact the Yiddish audience comes to the Yiddish theater precisely because they like it the way it is. Bunim illustrates his point with an anecdote:

"When they started performing the *Megile Songs* by Itsik Manger in Tel Aviv, the fans of the Burstein family (the Bursteins were the stars of the popular Yiddish theater) filled the theater. The stylized performance alienated them. When Mordecai took off his beard in front of the audience and moved to his next role as Haman, the audience suspected that the producers wanted to save money and made one actor play two roles. The production was on the brink of bankruptcy. Only after the critics praised it, and the more sophisticated public came to see it, the play became a hit."[22]

Bunim, in his version of the play also preferred to ignore the social criticism of the play. Bunim thought that the criticism Sholem Aleichem voiced over the predicament of the married woman in the orthodox Jewish community is nowadays relevant to a marginal group in society, and is of little interest to the general public.

## The Klezmer as an Artist

Although less than a hundred years separate us from the first performance of the play, contemporary directors regard Sholem Aleichem as a classic. Classic plays entail universal themes. The theme that mattered to Bunim in *Stempenyu* was the struggle for survival of the artist in society. For Bunim the axis, Rachel - Stempenyu, is not the backbone of the play. Rachel, in Bunim's opinion, is rather a pretext. Stempenyu wants to be free. Cheating on his wife, according to Bunim, was for Stempenyu a revolutionary act, a way to break the walls that surround him.

Both Rachel and Stempenyu are dissatisfied with their marriage, but for different reasons. For Rachel, Stempenyu is an exclusively romantic object. Whereas Stempenyu interweaves Rachel with his dream about a different, exciting life, far away from his depressing little town, in the big international music centers of Europe. For Stempenyu romantic élan and artistic dream mingle, and Rachel is perhaps the less important pull. Bunim cited the following scene to illustrate his point:

"Rachel: With me?

Stempenyu: With you...naturally. You should be free too, we should both be free as birds, we would be far away, away from the dirt...from the wild blind people...whose soul is only food, drink, sleep...They don't have a free moment, they don't know of any refined pleasures, they are blind, they don't see the beautiful world...They are deaf, they don't hear the beautiful tunes, they do not understand music...Music is a whole universe, a great wide new world!...Oh! If I could go and study music!...Play music.

Rachel: You have to study music?

Stempenyu: Naturally I have yet to study, study in a conservatory...It's a kind of school...a music academy. The best violinists study there, the best artists in the world! That's where the greatest people come from...I have been often told that if I study music, I'll be one of the greatest players in the world. A Paganini...

Rachel: A what?"[23]

Rachel is a pretext for Stempenyu, and the infidelity is an attempt to break loose, not only from his marriage but from the entire reality of the shtetl, beyond which there is a whole different world of art and spirituality. Bunim thought that this was the only interpretation that would make the play understandable to the audience today.

## The text of the playwright versus the text of the director

The motif of the alienated artist was not made up by Bunim. It appeared in the original Sholem Aleichem play. All Bunim had to do was to trim the Sholem Aleichem lines and give them more theatrical punch. We can see the touch of the director if we look at two passages. The first is from the original Sholem Aleichem text:

"Rachel: Where to?

Stempenyu: Far, far from here, there in the big, big world!...There we will live a free life...There I will throw away Stempenyu the Klezmer! I'll be famous! I'll be an artist. My name will be known in the entire world!

No more Stempenyu...I will be a Paganini! Did you hear of Paganini? I think I wrote you about Paganini!...

Rachel: And your wife? And my husband?

Stempenyu: What wife? What husband? Jews have such a thing as divorce. Follow me my soul. Rachel, the carriage is waiting for us... with everything I need. My violin and the notes...nothing more...All I need is you, my soul! You and my consolation, my violin."[24]

The following is the same passage edited by Bunim.

"Rachel: Leave me alone. Leave me...You are free as a bird, whereas I...Leave me...

Stempenyu: We will go away from here. Come let's go.

Rachel: (sadly) Where to?

Stempenyu: Wherever the horses will take us, come. The carriage is ready. It is waiting for us not far from here. It has everything in it.. the violin...the notes...everything!"[25]

A substantial difference in the working methods of the two could probably account for the better results achieved by Bunim. Sholem Aleichem worked at his desk, and once the play was finished he lost control of it. Bunim, on the other hand, used his adaptation only as a first draft, which then underwent many changes during rehearsals. Going over Bunim's prompt book one discovers that the above quoted dialogue between Rachel and Stempenyu was originally much longer and wordier. During the rehearsals it was pruned to the extent that more text was left out than left in.

## Bunim and the Role of the Jester

Bunim said of himself that he was always attracted to a theatrical theater, a non psychological, non realistic one. He liked the theater of Aristophanes, the Medieval theater, the comedia dell'arte: Theaters with naive theatrical elements. He then discovered that Jews also have a theatrical tradition of this kind: The *Purimshpil*. Since the *Purimshpil* was a street theater it needed an emcee as a mediator between the public and the comedians. The emcee would announce the beginning of the play and ask in flattering rhymes for payment towards its end. He would introduce the characters and comment on their good luck or misfortune. In a theater without a stage or stage design, he would explain the changes in scenery. Itsik Manger wrote his *Megile Songs* in the form of the Jewish folk theater, the *Purimshpil*.[26] Bunim got to know Manger's work in the fifties in Paris through a Yiddish puppet play based on Manger's *Midrash Itsik*.[27] The meeting between them resulted in the production of Manger's *Megile Songs* with Bunim as the director, first in Tel Aviv and then in New York. In the *Megile Songs* Bunim made extensive use of the *Purimshpil* technique including its use of the emcee.

Bunim thought that the technique of the *Purimshpil* was perfectly suited for a theatrical adaptation of *Stempenyu*. He looked in the cast for a character who could fulfil the function of the emcee. Bunim found him in the persona of the jester.

The ability of the jester to address himself directly to the audience, enabled Bunim to weave relevant passages from the novel into the play. The observations of the novelist were replaced by the comments of the jester.

Thus, the jester comments on the scene in the Jeweler shop. When the pleasure of receiving a gift becomes for her a nightmare, the jester is the only one who feels what Rachel is going through.

"Jester: *(to Rachel)* Everybody, Rachel, was embroiled in this necklace, Everybody...Moyshe Menashe among them. They fondled the pearls, weighed them, checked, smelled...and you Rachel, they forgot all about you, and nobody said, wear it well. *(Looks at her)* How beautiful the pearls lie around your neck...Wear them well, Rachel."[28]

What made the use of the jester so convincing was the fact that he was not a theatrical gimmick added to the play. He was one of the characters.

Film makers solve the problem of inserting a piece from the past into the present by means of the flashback. Instead, Bunim showed the audience how the unhappy marriage between Stempenyu and Freydl came about by using the jester and the musicians. They present the story of Stempenyu and Freydl as a play within a play.

## The play within the play

In the play within the play Bunim's direction reaches the highest degree of theatricality. The play within the play offers unlimited performing opportunities for the actor who plays the jester who in turn plays the female role of Freydl, or for the actor who plays the Klezmer who in turn plays Stempenyu.

The play within the play is performed in its entirety, including the female roles, by males. The theater shakes off for a minute its conventional image, and returns to the naive folk theater such as the comedia dell'arte or the *Purimshpil*.

In the *Purimshpil* the actor in the role of queen Vashti ties his beard. This is a sufficient indication that he is now female, as described in a short story by Sholem Aleichem:

"I envied Queen Vashti (played by Motl the Carpenter bedecked with a dress over his long black coat and with his beard tied with a kerchief) so that people should think he is a woman. I would have been just as happy to play Queen Esther played by Oyzer the Sexton's assistant who had a green apron around his hips. I would also be just as delighted to be in the shoes of Yoske the teacher's assistant who played the wicked Haman with a clay pot on his head."[29]

The scenery during the play within the play is simplified. Just like the *Purimshpil* it sheds curtains, painted back drops, revolving stages, and lighting effects. The stage design is a table:

"Mekhtche: (in the role of Stempenyu) What?...What is all this? What made you suddenly come here? (tries to climb on the table)

The Jester: (in the role of Freydl, grabbing Mekhtche by the pants) On my life! A good Question! Look at him, doesn't know from anything. Innocent as a corpse."[30]

This sequence is similar to the *Purimshpil* about the smugglers in Vonvild's Anthology of Yiddish folklore. There too the table constitutes the entire stage design. The Jewish smuggler hides under the table over which the Russian border policemen interrogates the landlord about him. The Jewish smuggler teases the Russian policeman crowing like a rooster from his shelter under the table.

"(The Customs Officer gets in and the smuggler hides under the table.)
Officer: Wasn't here a gentleman with foreign goods?
Landlord: He is not here.
Jew: Cock-a-doodle-do. I am too.
The officer starts looking for him and finds him under the table.
Officer: Your passport..."[31]

The Purimplayers, who went from house to house, used whatever furniture was available as scenery. In one of *The* Selling of Joseph plays, an upside down table with a white sheet on it, is the tomb of Rachel on which Joseph who was sold by his brothers to the Midianites laments his fate. Another player in the role of Rachel, Joseph's mother, is hiding under the same table and comforts Joseph from within the tomb.

"...After the Rabbis sat around, a table was put upside down in the middle of the room, covered with a white sheet, and the play began...The players won the hearts of the respectable public from the first moment, and when Joseph leaned back and rested his arm on his mother's grave and sang in a heartbreaking voice:

'Here every limb in my body is shivering

because this is my mother Rachel's tomb.'

And immediately afterwards cried out loud, 'Mother, Mother.' All the Rabbis began crying and people say that Rabbi Joshua Levin who was present at the performance almost lost his life because of the excitement."[32]

The endearing naiveté in the theatrical dresses and props of the *Purimshpil* would be kept in the play within the play. In another *Purimshpil* described by Sholem Aleichem a royal spectre is a long rod, covered with gold paper. The play within the play keeps the same *Purimshpil* spirit.

"Stempenyu's house. Shayke the bass player is disguised as a bride. Haykl the Jester is dressed in a skirt and wears a large kerchief on his head. Leybush the Clarinet player is crowned with a paper rooster. Mekhtche the Drummer is bedecked with a red ribbon on his neck and a squashed stovepipe hat. The smoke filled room is in disorder, and the four Klezmer are tipsy with wine. The scene continues:

All: (sing joyfully) Ho! What will become of us in this world and in the next! (They go on playing the story of Stempenyu and Freydl. Mekhtche is Stempenyu, and The Jester is Freydl. The rest accompany the performance with remarks, outbursts of laughter, questions: How did it happen? Why?

Shayke: A cake with raisins, black with green eyes.

(The Jester approaches, now in the role of Freydl, with Mekhtche around him.)

The Jester: What are you looking at me like that, Stempenyu! Don't you know me? Look how he wiggles his eyes like a tail. It's me, Freydl.

Mekhtche: Freydl? I know you are Freydl. What do you think I don't know? How did you get here Freydl?

The Jester: How? By foot, Stempenyu, and a little by coach.

Mekhtche: From where?

The Jester: Not from Jerusalem. From Home. Directly from home.

Mekhtche: From home? Well, what's new at your Mazepevke?

Jester: What can be new? Nothing is new.

Mekhtche: And how...how...say...was the fair?

Jester: This worries you a lot, Stempenyu, doesn't it? Without the 'fair' you can't fall asleep at night? (in a different tone -- straightforward) For six weeks we've been looking for you, we went everywhere, and each time the same story: 'Came and left'.

Mekhtche: Really... Huh.. And what made you come here? (tries to climb on the table)

Jester: (grabbing Mekhtche's pants) On my life I could swear it's a good question! Look at him, doesn't know a thing. Innocent like a corpse.

Mekhtche: Listen Freydl, I have no patience for riddles. I ask you what are you doing here, and you answer me in riddles. (tries to climb on the table. Freydl stops him.)"[33]

Stempenyu tries to get rid of Freydl, but finally gives in and marries her. The play within the play ends in a *Purimshpil*-like parody of the wedding ceremony.

"Jester: Lend me one ear and I'll tell you something...It might change your mind!

Voices: Lend her an ear Stempenyu...Lend her an ear...

(Mekhtche bends his head and the Jester whispers something in his ear, and at the same time shows with a movement of the hands that he is pregnant. The Klezmer burst out in loud laughter. They sing a parody of the traditional Jester song: 'Cry, Bridegroom, Cry.'

Klezmer: Cry, Bridegroom, cry.

(The wedding ceremony starts, the wedding dance begins. Enter Stempenyu.)

Mekhtche: Stempenyu! Where have you been Stempenyu? Where did you go?"[34]

In the play within the play Bunim gives the audience all the background information it needs by cleverly using the dramatic potential of the Klezmer.

## Toning down the Schmaltz

The shortcomings of Sholem Aleichem's dramatization are apparent in the treatment of Chaya Etel. Chaya Etel became important in the dramatic adaptation. Bunim at first followed Sholem Aleichem. In the first draft of his adaptation as in that of Sholem Aleichem, Chaya Etel became the heroine of a parallel plot. Bunim maintained, as did Sholem Aleichem in his foreword to the novel, that Stempenyu was a story that could indeed have happened, that Rachel and Stempenyu could have really existed. The *shtetl* (Jewish small town) existed. In the novel, Sholem Aleichem described reality the way it was, even if the result was less thrilling than the cheap novels à la Shomer. This is why the character of Chaya Etel finally did not comply with Bunim's realistic concept of the play. Bunim wanted a play with realistic contents. The ghost of Chaya Etel went beyond the frame he set for himself. From here it was but one step to give up on her completely. Paradoxically, by changing his play, Bunim remained faithful to the original intention of Sholem Aleichem. In his foreword to the novel Sholem Aleichem wrote:

"My intention was to create three characters in this novel, or as they call them, 'main characters': the Jewish artist Stempenyu with his violin, the Jewish woman Rachel the beautiful with her Jewish honesty, and the Jewish wife Freydl, with her mercantile spirit, and her shaking over the ruble - each with their particular world. Stempenyu, Rachel and Freydl - those are the main passengers who sit up in the best seats, and all the rest are no more than side characters, second class passengers so to speak. That's why I got rid of the other characters with a few words, and dedicated my entire labor to those privileged three".[35]

Giving up on Chaya Etel did not harm the play. If anything, Bunim prevented the play from sliding into the melodramatic pattern of Sholem Aleichem's adaptation.

## Dénouement

The dénouement is similar in Bunim and in Sholem Aleichem's adaptation. Rachel drowns herself. Bunim maintained that Rachel and Stempenyu were two characters out of the ordinary. They were different than all the other characters of the shtetl. This is why Bunim was not afraid of such a melodramatic ending. However, the same end gets a different meaning in the two dramatic adaptations. In Sholem Aleichem's version Stempenyu loses his mind. The heavily loaded play ends with a strong melodramatic climax. Bunim ends with an anticlimax. In Bunim's play, after the end comes an epilogue. The epilogue brings us back to the insipid daily life of the shtetl. By means of the epilogue Bunim shows how life is back to normal. The same futile conversations take place at the same street corners. A tragedy took place but it is not going to change anything. By showing that the tragedy did not really touch anybody Bunim made it even greater.

## *Problems of Translation*

In his quest for linguistic raw materials Sholem Aleichem enjoyed the role of the ethnographer. In the novel *Moshkele the Thief [Moshkele Ganev]*[36] he compiled the vocabulary of the thieves. In *Stempenyu* he brought a selected choice from the language of the Klezmer.

Bunim and his co-writer Shabtay, did not have a Hebrew equivalent for the Yiddish idiom. Modern Hebrew has an array of professional jargons. The jargon of the military, of the taxi drivers, etc. There is no Hebrew, or for that matter English Klezmer jargon. Sholem Aleichem could draw from an authentic Klezmer jargon and feed his characters with idiomatic expressions. Bunim and Shabtay had to make something out of nothing. The two succeeded to create a linguistic fiction, a mimesis to a non existent language of non existing Klezmer. Berkowitz in his translation of the novel[37] tried to give a Hebrew equivalent to the Klezmer jargon, but his product was too literary. It has verbal panache, but lacks the directness of authentic spoken Hebrew. Shabtay took another direction. He did not try to translate. He did not look for Hebrew equivalents to the original Yiddish expressions. Instead he created new verbal combinations. In his adaptation Shabtay created a fictional idiomatic language. When Stempenyu in his adaptation says: "They are blind like a wheel of a coach" or when Freydl says "Look how his eyes wiggle like a tail" it sounds like folk language without really being one.

## Bunim Directs *Stempenyu* in New York

The Folksbine theater invited Bunim to direct *Stempenyu*. The Folksbine, since its foundation in 1915, presented a literary repertoire which means in the Yiddish theater, plays by playwrights of the better category as opposed to the repertoire of the cheap commercial theater. While working with the ensemble Bunim discovered that the tradition of the Yiddish theater prevails in an artistic theater like the Folksbine as well. The Folksbine actors showed complete disrespect for team work, and the stage discipline it implies.

Yiddish actors, as Bunim soon found out, and this applied to the Folksbine actors as well, are not used to stage discipline. They ignore for example the time limits in which an actor says a line. In the Yiddish theater there is no tempo. Even if he has only one line, a Yiddish actor will make a dish out of it. He will take his time before saying it, in the middle he will take a break, sigh, and so on. The actor in the Yiddish theater cannot grasp his role as a part of an overall picture on the stage. In scenes where he is supposed to be in the background, he will try somehow to attract attention. When a Yiddish actor has a line, the stage is his. He speaks. And if another actor - even by order of the director - does something on stage, it bothers him. As a rule, Yiddish actors are used to unlimited freedom, and adapt with difficulty, if at all, to the work with a director.

The traditional Yiddish theater worked, and still does, by the star system. The star is a popular, bankable actor, who gathers around him a troupe that he rules with an iron hand. Since every actor keeps in his heart the stardom dream, and is in his own eyes a potential star, there is no basis or willingness for team work. In the commercial theater the star pushes the troupe to the background. Since the star is often also the owner, the other actors must comply. In a subsidized theater like the Folksbine, where the actors do not fear the star, each actor pulls the play in his direction. This way, when an actor speaks, instead of speaking to his partner, he talks to the audience. The actors feel independent of the rest. Even in the middle of a dialogue the actors manage to flirt with the audience. As Bunim puts it: "There are no dialogues. Only monologues. It's my turn! Now me!"[38] In his work on Sholem Aleichem's text, Bunim wanted to follow the footsteps of the Russian Director Dicky, who directed an innovative version of *The Treasure* in the Hebrew national theater Habima in 1928. Dicky succeeded in breaking the *krekhts*, the Jewish sigh, on stage. In pouring old wine into a new pitcher Dicky created a modern Sholem Aleichem performance. However this happened in the more sophisticated Hebrew theater. In the Yiddish theater, actors and spectators are unwilling to accept change. The public in the Folksbine would not accept that Stempenyu talks to Rachel through a window, and there is no window on stage. In the Habima production there was no window. They acted a window. On the Yiddish stage the actors and the public do not accept the use of theatrical suggestions. A wall must be a wall. Understatement, or stylized acting are not accepted. *Stempenyu*, Bunim believes, must be played with allusions, stylization, self control. A difficult assignment, to which Yiddish actors are not accustomed. Apparently there was no change in the acting on the Yiddish stage, when it comes to plays from the Jewish repertoire in the 30 years that separate the presentation of Stempenyu in the Folksbine with Bunim, and the Stempenyu of the Yiddish Art Theater [Yidisher Kunst Teater] in the adaptation and participation of Maurice Schwartz. The critic of the New York Times wrote on the 29th of March 1929:

"When the play (*Stempenyu*) started, there was some pretense at acting, but as it progressed and volley after volley of humor was fired on the stage, the audience worked itself into such continuous laughter that the cast got the infection. All the restraint of the memorable acting of 'The Cherry Orchard' was thrown to the winds. Art was forgotten and the play became a turmoil: Arms waved, voices rose to a high pitch, and the rollicking songs became more rollicking. Mr. Schwartz as the husband, kept his poise, and so did Rachel played by Miss Celia Adler, and the audience enjoyed it all hugely, and for a theater audience to have a good time is a worst, only second to art."[39]

## The critics in Tel Aviv

The press reacted to the play varied from absolute praise to total disapproval. Mr. Ben Ami in *Maariv* had nothing but praise for the production. The critic praised the very initiative of presenting a play from the Jewish repertoire, since "it is an important deed in the complex endeavor of inheriting national consciousness to the public at large, and to the youth in particular." [40]

The critic praised the director:

"Like Sholem Aleichem Bunim tackled the subject matter and the characters with the tender approach of a lover - and he managed to communicate this feeling to the audience, in presenting a sparkling, flowing, pleasurable performance."[41]

The acting too, was according to Mr. Ben Ami flawless:

"The actors deserve all praise, some for a character role some for a local flavor roles, and the main thing, that they were all organically interwoven harmonically in the general atmosphere of the play."[42]

The composer (Dov Seltzer) and the painter-designer (Arieh Navon) succeeded in creating a refined background that added a lot to the performance, according to Mr. Ben Ami.

Ms. Zartal in the daily <u>Davar</u> gave her article the title "Watered Down Folklore". She explained:

"The dramatic material that Bunim tackled in the Sholem Aleichem play *Stempenyu* is not of high quality. It is a very small melodrama, flat, not crystallized, although it is based on a charming story."[43]

The director's approach was also wrong. Ms. Zartal mentioned two possible interpretations to the play. The first one was to put on a play in the old melodramatic tradition of the Yiddish theater.

"Choosing deliberately this direction could achieve two goals simultaneously - depicting the folklore of the shtetl and reconstructing a theatrical style that no longer exists."[44]

The other possibility was to emphasize and deepen the social aspect of the play. Sharpen the confrontation between the materialistic provincial bourgeoisie on the one hand, and the carefree Klezmer that live an alternative life of freedom and creativity on the other hand. Bunim's mistake was, according to Ms. Zartal, his inability to chose between the two.

"He tried to create folkloristic images of the shtetl. He wanted to tell the private story of Stempenyu and Rachel, and with it incorporate the social content. The result is neither fish nor fowl."[45]

The performance ended up being incoherent. The actors gave a fine performance although the directing was deficient and in spite of the fact that:

"The characters of Sholem Aleichem in the play are shallow. The dialogues are flat and unable to explain the human situation depicted in the play and the terrible complications that trap the characters."[46]

Boaz Evron dealt in his article with the problem of presenting Sholem Aleichem to a contemporary audience. Bunim, wrote Evron, took advantage of Sholem Aleichem's *forte*, his descriptive talent:

"Shmuel Bunim, in his interpretation of Sholem Aleichem's Stempenyu, in the lively clever linguistic adaptation of Shabtay in 'Habima', created rather than a dramatic play, a series of tableaux of the Jewish *shtetl*, orchestrated and stylized in choreographic precision, with humor and restraint."[47]

Bunim, Evron went on, succeeded in using the shund element which is antithetically contained in the Sholem Aleichem text, and presented it from an angle of a amused irony. Evron thought that the actors in the roles of Stempenyu and Rachel created rather flat characters. On the other hand, in a stylized and theatrical performance of this kind, one could not linger on the psychological aspect of the characters. This is also the reason why Evron rejected the brusque, melodramatic dénouement of the performance. Rachel in Bunim's version, found escape in suicide. The overdramatic ending got the play into a confusion of styles. Evron wrote:

"The dramatic-linear element was almost hidden under the series of the beautifully stylized images, so that Rachel's suicide came as a complete surprise because there was no real development leading to it, and it does not shake us up. It is accidental, because we did not get to know her as a dramatic-tragic character. We enjoy more the pranks of the jester, in the beautifully agile performance of Rafael Klatchkin, or the generously comical character of Ada Tal in the role of the mother in law, or the ill tempered grumbling of Leo Yung in the role of her husband, and the performance of most of the other participants.

Thus, Bunim created a charming performance, however somewhat blurred, because of the two elements which did not reach a proper synthesis."[48]

## *Stempenyu* – Epilogue

*Stempenyu*, the play, did not become the model for the "Jewish play," the counterpart of the "Jewish novel" in the theater. The reasons for that were to be found both in Sholem Aleichem, and in the Yiddish theater in New York where he worked.

Sholem Aleichem had a fresh and unique approach to the novel. In his novels he looked for and indeed found a voice of his own. He was less confident in his approach to playwriting. His starting position was a reservation about the existing theater rather than a vision of a new one. Sholem Aleichem wanted to populate the Yiddish stage with characters who had strong stage presence. However a character, or even a few characters, do not make up a theatrical style. This does not mean that a playwright must publish a detailed theatrical manifesto, like Brecht for example, in order to write a drama. But a playwright should know where he stands in the theater, he should have a definite concept of his kind of theater. Goldfaden never reached the literary level of Sholem Aleichem, but Goldfaden created his own theatrical style: A set of theatrical tableaux, romantic dialogues, a mix of upstairs and downstairs scenes, and a string of theatrical effects such as fireworks, complete with song and dance, that end many of his plays. That is why the Goldfaden comedy is always theatrically alive. *Stempenyu* took over quite a few of the characteristics of the shund drama, which the writer had so vehemently opposed. It would be unfair to put the entire blame for the failure of the 1907 production on Sholem Aleichem. The change in the character of the work came about in a large measure through external, non-artistic factors. *Stempenyu*, the novel, was written by Sholem Aleichem, who was then a young millionaire, and a patron of the arts. By the time he began working on adapting it for the stage, Sholem Aleichem was sick, preoccupied with financial problems and the burden of a big family. He was now dependent on the stars of the Yiddish stage for his livelihood. Art was not their primary concern. *Stempenyu* did not become a model for the "Jewish play" or the continuation of the "Jewish novel" in the theater, largely because Sholem Aleichem the playwright did not have the same degree of artistic freedom he had as a novelist.

He was not given the opportunity to polish his plays in a theater, with actors. The Molieresque comedy is the fruit of twenty years work with a wandering troupe in the French Provinces, a close contact with the Italian comedians, and more years of work under the auspices of the royal family. Only after years of failure as a writer of tragedies and the continuous day to day contact with the theater, actors, and public, did Molière gradually, in fact unwillingly, discover his true genius. As a matter of fact Molière thought himself to be a tragedian for two decades. Sholem Aleichem, the playwright, had to enter the theater like the goddess Athena, in a complete and perfect shape from the first minute he made an appearance on the Jewish stage. He never had the last word in the production of his plays either. When *Stempenyu* was staged in Thomashefsky's People's Theater, the artistic decisions were made by others, and this probably contributed to the weakness of the dramatic adaptation. It seems that Sholem Aleichem was aware of the problem. For long years he hoped for and worked for the establishment of a Jewish theater, for which he could write his plays. In an optimistic letter written in 1905 he writes to his daughter Ernestina about an agreement reached between himself and the directors Spivakovsky and Adler about founding an artistic Yiddish theater in Odessa. Berkowitz who published the letter in *The Sholem Aleichem Book*[49] added that the contract between them had already been signed, but in the end nothing came out of it. Spoilers hinted to the Russian authorities that the new theater would have revolutionary tendencies, and the whole enterprise was ended before it began.

Most probably if *Stempenyu* had been presented in the Yiddish artistic theater that never came to life in Odessa, it would have been completely different from the *Stempenyu* of the People's Theater. In New York the playwright always had an inferior status in the Jewish theatrical community, and Sholem Aleichem was no exception to the rule.

Shmuel Bunim confronted in his interpretation a problem that Sholem Aleichem could not solve: The transition from the novel to the play. Bunim brought back to the play the folksy charm of the novel by using the model of the *Purimshpil*. Another element that was lost in the transition from the novel to the play was the intimacy between the author and his public. In the novel Sholem Aleichem addressed himself every now and then to his public, his "Dear Readers". He established an intimate link with his readers, bypassing the story and its characters. In the play the direct address to the audience was lost. The use of the jester, as a possible channel for the participation of the author in the play, would have enabled Sholem Aleichem to be as warm and engaging in his play as he was in his novel. Bunim recreated this intimacy in his adaptation. The *Purimshpil* enabled him to draw the best from the play with the best from the novel and organize them into one theatrical entity.

A comparative reading in the novel and the play, both by Sholem Aleichem shows that the play is a pale reflection of the novel. Like Sholem Aleichem's adaptation before him, Bunim's adaptation did not succeed in structuring a convincing plot. Rachel's suicide towards the end of the play seems to be out of context. However Bunim gave beautiful theatrical answers to the problems presented by the Sholem Aleichem text. He used the theatricality of the Sholem

Aleichem characters, and presented a series of beautiful stylized tableaux. Furthermore, the brilliance of Bunim does not come from the outside. The theatricality of the performance was built with the materials he found in the original Sholem Aleichem work and in the Jewish folklore that inspired it. *Stempenyu* by **Bunim** comes under the category of Jewish theater that Sholem Aleichem dreamt of creating.

## 4. The Treasure

The treasure motif has a significant place in Sholem Aleichem's work. Dreams of fortune have always been part of poverty-stricken societies. Tales of big wins, lotteries, and treasures were popular among the destitute Jews of Eastern Europe. In Sholem Aleichem's work, dreams about a sudden salutary fortune appear time and again. Sometimes it is as an individual dream like that of Menachem Mendel or Shimele Saroker, and at times it is a collective fantasy like in *The Treasure*.

Sholem Aleichem was ambivalent about the treasure motif. He was both fascinated and weary of it. On the one hand the treasure legends were kept deep in his heart, and accompanied him all his life. On the other hand he saw in them the cause for the passivity and economic decline of the Jews. The following is a passage from his story, *The Treasure*:

"But my brothers in Mazepevke have confidence unparalleled elsewhere in the world. The inhabitants of this dead valley still sit expecting miracles, waiting for fried pigeons to fly right into their mouths."[1]

Sholem Aleichem experienced personally the transition from acute poverty to legendary fortune and back. When he started writing he was a young millionaire and a benefactor of struggling Jewish writers. In the impoverished literary circles, legend had it that he rolled cigars with shiny crisp hundred ruble bills. Before long he lost his fortune in the stock market and joined the ranks of his needy fellow writers.

Sholem Aleichem's attitude towards dreams of big fortune kept swinging like a pendulum between logic and emotion, between the brain and the heart, while the heart as Pascal knew, has a logic of its own.[2]

In the play we find the two conflicting attitudes side by side.

Benny, The young American farmer, is presented as a role model in contrast to the economically backwards *shtetl* Jews. A farmer was the best symbol of a productive person Sholem Aleichem could think of.

On the other hand, the exaltation brought about by the irrational belief in the treasure is described with sympathy. Although it leads nowhere, the belief in the treasure brings comfort and a taste of sweetness to the desolate life of the *shtetl* Jews.

The interpretations of the various directors would also echo this ambivalence, and move back and forth between the two attitudes. One director would come up with a critical, satiric interpretation, and another with a sentimental, lyrical one.

## The Making of the Play

In February of 1908 Sholem Aleichem wrote from Berlin to Berkowitz, his son in law in New York, about *The Treasure*, a new comedy he had just written. When he returned from Berlin to Geneva, Sholem Aleichem wanted to try out the new comedy on an audience. He read it for a group of Russian Jews who were mainly students and political refugees. Encouraged by the audience's warm reception, Sholem Aleichem sent the manuscript to Berkowitz so that he would sell it to the actor that he valued most, Jacob Adler. In a cover letter to the manuscript Sholem Aleichem wrote:

"Today I send you my *Treasure*. And treasure it is. As soon as you get it go to the big eagle...[The actor Adler whose last name means eagle, J.W.] I am sure that he will accept it immediately. Observe his reaction to the reading of the play...If it is very positive, ask for an immediate down payment of two thousand dollars. And if his reaction is moderate (which I doubt), fifteen hundred...and then play it by ear. Naturally it would be better to leave him the *Treasure* for a few days and wait for him to reach for you and beg. But alas, we sit here with hardly any pennies left. So don't leave him empty handed."[3]

Berkowitz read the play for Adler, and it first seemed as if Adler intended to buy it for his theater. In the end however, he changed his mind. Adler rejected the play for two reasons: First, he did not want to play the role he considered to be the best, Holovshke the policeman, because the character had converted to Christianity. In a young theater, such as the Yiddish theater at the turn of the century, the public often confused the actor with the part he played. In the history of theater we know of cases where outraged spectators hurt and even killed the stage villain. In the Jewish theater the spectators stopped short of such violence and contented themselves by booing or giving the actors the benefit of their advice. The actors too felt personally involved in the roles they played.

Giving the best role to another actor was also ruled out, because he might steal the show.

Adler's second argument was more relevant. He felt that from a dramatic point of view the play left much to be desired. Although the dialogues and scenes were well written, they were not structured in one tightly knit plot. Furthermore, the play was not built around one super role. Adler could function only in a play built around one main part, his own. Adler's disappointment with *The Treasure* was understandable. The play did have a role for him, but what of it if the other roles were just as attractive? Adler expressed his discontent to Berkowitz:

"Here in *The Treasure* I don't have even one worthwhile role. Just speeches and speeches. Moskowitz will get the best part: Holoveshke the convert. That is the only living part in the entire play. At least he is doing something, and later on, the spectators will quote his Russian sayings in all the sweatshops on the east side...I would be delighted to play the role of Holoveshke, but it would be improper for me to play the part of a convert. Don't forget that I am the great Adler!"[4]

Although Sholem Aleichem was easily influenced, and willingly accepted criticism, he refused to bury *The Treasure* in a drawer. Berkowitz described his feelings:

"Sholem Aleichem who wrote his dramatic pieces so easily, and sometimes left them just as easily, or even burnt them (if the 'connoisseurs' did not approve of them), did not want to leave *The Treasure* alone, and could not free himself from it. Deep in his heart he believed that this time he had come up with a great theatrical work, and considered the failure of the play with the New York theater crowd as a horrid injustice, an inexplicable sin, and the result of the low level of the Yiddish theater."[5]

The humiliating attitude of the Jewish theater people in New York (Thomashefsky and Kessler also turned down the play) caused Sholem Aleichem great pain, but he went on believing in the play, working on it, and polishing it.

In the meantime Dovid Pinsky published a play called *The Treasure* and Sholem Aleichem decided to avoid confusion and call the second and final version of his play *The Gold Diggers*.

Both manuscripts are kept in the Sholem Aleichem House in Tel Aviv.

In the first version of the play called *The Treasure* one notices dramatic flaws that were corrected in the second version, *The Gold Diggers*.

The first version is wordier. The dialogues resemble a succession of monologues that the characters recite in turn. In the second version Sholem Aleichem cut entire portions that were not essential to the dramatic action. He seemed to be more aware of the time limitations of the stage as well as the need for dramatic suspense.

The dénouement too, is more dramatic in the second version. Benny impersonates a ghost who convinces Esther's father to allow their marriage. In the first version, for no apparent dramatic reason, Benny reveals his charade. In the second version the practical joke is discovered in a dramatic confrontation, when Holoveshke feels cheated by Benny and squeals on him.

*The Treasure* and *The Gold Diggers* bear no substantial thematic differences. Their difference lies only in the improved dramatic technique of the later version. One can see why Berkowitz chose to publish the second version of the play in the Yiddish literary magazine <u>Di Zukunft</u>.[6] When Berkowitz published Sholem Aleichem's works in Hebrew, he again chose the second version.[7] In the preface to the play Berkowitz asserted that Sholem Aleichem himself preferred this version.

### The Third Version – An Attempt at a New Genre

As a young millionaire Sholem Aleichem founded and financed a Yiddish literary magazine: The Jewish Folk Library [Di Yidishe Folksbibliotek]. His goal was to enable the publication of literary works in Yiddish, works that stood in opposition to the cheap sensational taste of the commercial publishers. Sholem Aleichem's fortune disappeared in the stock market and the self financed *The Jewish Folk Library* with it.

Twenty years later, in 1908 young Yiddish writers in Vilna started a new literary magazine <u>Literary Monthly</u> [<u>Literarishe Monatsshriftn</u>]. Nothing could be closer to Sholem Aleichem's heart than this literary venture. He decided to rework *The Treasure* for publication in the young avant-garde monthly. Berkowitz wrote about the third version of the play:

"Not only two treasures – Sholem Aleichem wrote a third treasure. The third version came to the world following a literary event, that excited the Yiddish Literary circles of that time. There appeared in Vilna the magazine <u>Literary Monthly</u> [<u>Literarishe Monatsshriftn</u>]) which meant to open a new chapter in the young and growing Yiddish literature. Three young writers, A. Veiter, S. Niger, and S. Gorelik, all three veterans of the big political turmoil in Vilna, finally rid themselves of the various sectarian socialist ideologies, and united in an effort to create a new style in the Yiddish literature and elevate it from its low, popular level, to the high standards of the 'intelligentsia.' One of the three editors, S. Gorelik, came to Geneva, and brought with him the first copies of the magazine. Sholem Aleichem looked with longing at the new monthly in which he saw a later development of his youthful endeavor, *The Jewish Folk*

*Library* [Di Yidishe Folksbibliotek], and a secret desire to take part in the young, fresh magazine came over him. Since at that time he was absorbed with his *Treasure*, a new idea crossed his mind, to make a third adaptation of the comedy, a modern one, and he proceeded immediately..."[8]

The first issue of the magazine published Peretz's play, In the Synagogue Anteroom - *A Thing in Three Acts*.[9] The dialogues in Peretz's play were written in a poetic style, and almost all the characters were nameless symbolic figures such as: A Sinner, A Madman, A Loose Woman, A Coachman, A Rabbi, Musicians, Butchers, and Landlords. Sholem Aleichem followed Peretz's footsteps. In the third version he changed the individual names of his characters to their symbolic designations. Levi Mozgovyer was renamed Busybody, Wlozlawsky became Polish Landowner, and Yidl the Bag became Money Lender. Sholem Aleichem opened the play with a grim tableau. The *shtetl's* carefree poverty was turned into a melancholy picture of sordid misery.

"Third Pair: Have compassion for a poor invalid with one leg. (shows his crutches) You will earn a *mitzvah*.

Fourth Pair: This you call an invalid? That is an invalid. (shows a handicapped person with crooked hands and legs bent by some terrible deficiency) This poor soul is mine. I should get your charity, I should get more than anyone else. Just look at him."[10]

The invalids remind us of the Breughelian lame beggars in the opening scene of Peretz's play:

"On the bench in front of the synagogue lies the lame one, with his head in the blind man's lap. Poor people come by..."[11]

Peretz established a clear affinity between the abstract designations of the characters and the text they deliver.

"Lame One: Had feet - ran to evil!

Blind Man: The agents of evil - eyes!

A Poor Man: Ate at Rabbi Bracha's table.

Second Poor Man: Friday night - money for the bathhouse, and a shirt, and a dress...

Madman: Better - free room and board."[12]

Unlike Peretz Sholem Aleichem was not consistent. His characters were meant to be symbolic, but the text that they delivered was realistic, and lacked the poetic and allegoric dimensions that characterized Peretz's play.

At first it seemed as though Sholem Aleichem had adopted a new dramatic style in the vein of the young literary magazine. However the changes were merely on the surface, and left the essence of the play untouched. Sholem Aleichem's attempt to write a symbolist drama proved that this literary genre was alien to him, if not as a reader, then as a writer.

In the third version Sholem Aleichem emphasized the ideological message of the play. He emphasized the credo that disunity among the Jews is the cause of their misfortune.

This was not a new idea in Sholem Aleichem's writings. It had appeared in the Hebrew story *The Treasure* twenty years earlier in 1889, and reappeared in the two previous versions of the play. In the early versions of the play however the ideological message was lost in the colorful loud brouhaha of the plot. Only in the third version it was brought to the forefront. Sholem Aleichem added a scene where a group of beggars appear in the cemetery and demand their share in the treasure. In a sequence that echoed the revolutionary spirit of the time (1908), the graveyard became a battlefield between the *sans culottes* and the rich.

In keeping with the ideological tone of the new version Sholem Aleichem got rid of the romantic plot. Molière, the father of modern European comedy, used the pretext of a romantic plot to unmask social evils. So did Sholem Aleichem in the first version of *The Treasure*. In the third version of *The Treasure* the ideological conflict took the shape of an open and direct confrontation between the allegorical characters without the cushioning device of the romantic plot.

### The Ambivalent Attitude Toward America

Sholem Aleichem used Benny as a positive model in opposition to the collective delusion about the treasure. Benny is the Jewish farmer from America who acts instead of dreaming. However the sympathy Sholem Aleichem felt for the pragmatic American was somewhat reserved. In a letter to Berkowitz he apologized for his reservation about the character:

"It's not that Benny is such a boaster, or a bluffer, he is rather a plain, uneducated guy."[13]

The fault that Sholem Aleichem found with him is his simple mindedness. Indeed Benny is a mixture of practical sense and spiritual rawness. Those were symbiotic attributes in Sholem Aleichem's eyes. The opposing symmetry in Levi Mozgovyer bears witness to it. Mozgovyer is a combination of spiritual richness and inadequacy in practical matters. The same pattern is repeated in *The Jackpot*. The tailor Shimele Saroker has no practical sense and a vivid imagination, whereas the landlord Fein has practical sense and a dull mind.

Benny, the practical American could not fit into the third version. This poetic version of the play does not deal with concrete issues such as the productivity prospects of Eastern European Jewry. In the third version Sholem Aleichem does not shuttle between the two contradictory attitudes towards the treasure. He decides in favor of the dream.

## *The Treasure* – A Model for a Jewish Play

In a letter dated November 1908 Sholem Aleichem wrote to the star of the Yiddish theater Jacob Adler about his latest comedy, *The Treasure*:

"My good friend and great artist Adler!

I give you my most recent work *The Treasure*. I can say to you two words - it is for you a treasure!... I shall not and I must not tell you any more. Those who heard it, say that this is the first Jewish, genuinely Jewish comedy! I am more than convinced, that you will have nothing but words of thanks for *The Treasure*. Naturally you must play the role of Levy Mozgovyer...This is a character that only you can interpret correctly. He is not an idiot, he is not, as some may think, a fool, but a Jew who has faith. Chew him properly and you will create a great thing."[14]

The letter is interesting for two reasons. Sholem Aleichem considered the possibility that *The Treasure* represented a theatrical breakthrough: it was the first of its kind "Jewish comedy." Sholem Aleichem thought that he is about to revolutionize the Yiddish theater the way he revolutionized Yiddish literature. *The Treasure* he believed could do what *Stempenyu* failed to do a year earlier: Rid the Yiddish stage of the Shund, and create a world class Jewish theater.

A second significant point in Sholem Aleichem's letter to Adler pertains to the nature of the new "Jewish Comedy." In his letter to Adler Sholem Aleichem does not refer to the plot, the comic situations, dramatic reversals, or the visual comic elements. The only thing on his mind were the characters. *The Treasure* which Sholem Aleichem considered without false modesty to be the model for the future genre of the Jewish Comedy, is a comedy of characters. Although it has dramatic turns, it does not aspire to be a comedy of surprises à la Ben Johnson. Sholem Aleichem's interest in the plot was secondary. The dramatic conflict was for him only a vehicle to carry his gallery of characters. The aim was the creation of a vital space for the Jewish character, the Sholem Aleichem Jewish character. Indeed, different interpretations of Sholem Aleichem's plays focused on the characters. Changes in the plot left little mark on the plays. The resolution of the conflict was also secondary. In Sholem Aleichem's words, the director and the actors had to properly chew the *characters* in order to create a great thing.

### Berkowitz Changes the Play

In his preface to the Hebrew adaptation Berkowitz mentions adding new characters to the play:

"Thus I introduced dramatis personae to *The Treasure*, characters that did not appear in the original, such as Lazer Wolf, and Shimon Eli, Sholem the Matchmaker, Arieh the Undertaker, Feiga Lea, and others, that were originally created by the writer in different pieces, such as in *Tevye the Dairyman*, *The Bewitched Tailor*, *Divorce*, *There are No Dead Ones*, and *Motl the Cantor's Son*".[15]

Some of the characters, such as Arieh the Undertaker, or Shimon Eli, proved their theatrical vitality, perhaps thanks to the masterful performances of actors like Klatchkin and Friedland, in the Habima performance of 1928. Secondly, and Berkowitz is the first to admit it, those characters too are the creation of Sholem Aleichem, and have the Sholem Aleichem charm. The transition from the literature to drama did not harm them, since Sholem Aleichem's stories often use direct speech, and are easily adaptable to the theater.

The fact that Berkowitz could add half a dozen characters to the play without basically altering it, justifies the definition of the Sholem Aleichem comedy and particularly *The Treasure*, as a gallery of characters.

However, Berkowitz did more than add characters to the play. He changed the characters, thus damaging the delicate nucleus of the play.

Sholem Aleichem ignored the convention of comedy that implies the division of the characters into good and bad. Nor was he interested in the victory of the good over the bad. Berkowitz wanted the good to win.

In order for the good hero to win, the comedy from Terence to Molière, provides him with secondary characters, whose only purpose is to help him overcome the villain. The original play did not have auxiliary characters. Berkowitz took characters from the original play and made secondary characters out of them. Holovshke was the principal victim of this change. In Russian Goloveshke means a burning ash. In the original play Holoveshke gets caught in the treasure fever. The ash in the heart of the old constable turns into fire. Holoveshke wants to get married to Esther, the beautiful daughter of Levy Mozgovyer. In the Berkowitz adaptation Holoveshke has no dreams of his own. He becomes a mere instrument in Benny's scheme to win Esther.

Berkowitz minimized the weight of the secondary roles and empowered of the pivotal characters who advanced the plot. Thus Berkowitz gives Benny more guts, he becomes a fighter, a Jewish

American patriot, the avenger of his people. In the following passage he defends Esther's honor.

"Wlozlawsky: (Turns up his moustache. Makes a bow) Please, Mrs. Esterka, I kneel before you. (tries to kiss her hand) I kiss your little hands, beautiful bride. (Esther hides her hands and Wlozlawsky pinches her cheek.)

Benny: Hey, Mister, take your hands off! (slaps him on the hand and pushes him from Esther.)

Wlozlawski: (enraged) You son of a bitch. *Zhid*! (kike) I am a Pole!

Benny: What did you say? *Zhid*? Just say that once more! (shows him his fist) You God damned fool! I am an American! I'll show you what *Zhid* means!"[16]

Towards the end of the play Berkowitz makes Benny the savior of the town. He prevents the construction of a railroad through the Jewish cemetery. He also leaves a handsome sum of money before departing with Esther. Benny is no doubt a better match for Esther than the constable Holoveshke, but the struggle between them was hardly the center of the original play. Sholem Aleichem would not give Holoveshke his comical Russian sayings which made him the darling of the audience if all he wanted was to present him as an unworthy contender for Ester.

Unlike the comedy writers of the Haskala Sholem Aleichem avoided the cliché of the positive hero who confronts and overcomes an evil antagonist, the representative of an ignorant, backward society.

The Sholem Aleichem comedy is not an ideological battlefield that ends with the definite victory of light over darkness, the learned over the ignorant, the good over the bad.

Berkowitz's attempt to put Benny on the right side of such a conflict appears, therefore, both tasteless and needless.

## Dicky Versus Berkowitz

The production of *The Treasure* by the Russian director Dicky in Habima in 1928 is still considered to be the most remarkable of all.

Dicky used a Berkowitz adaptation, but he changed it radically. In his preface to the Hebrew translation of the play Berkowitz wrote: "I here take the opportunity to draw your attention to the fact that the version of *The Treasure* in this book, is utterly different from the version performed by the Habima Theater. Not only in that this version contains four acts (as opposed to three in the Habima version), but it is different in its very structure in the development of the plot, and in the nature of the characters."[17]

One senses that Berkowitz was not pleased with the version of the play performed in Habima.

The first noticeable thing we encounter in Dicky's stage version is the faster pace of the play. Dicky shortened the play by one act. In the remaining text he left only dialogues that enhanced the action on stage.

Berkowitz opened the play in Levy Mozgovyer's house. A few of the townspeople sit there in order to keep an eye on him so that he will not abscond with the treasure. Dicky thought that the opening scene of a comedy whose protagonist is the whole community, should cover the entire stage. Just like Sholem Aleichem Dicky opened with a picture of the market place. The vendors stand behind their shabby pushcarts. In the middle of the market place Shimon Eli (Klatchkin) sat on the stub of a tree trunk dressed in rags, humming a melancholy Hasidic tune while mending torn clothes. The actor Chemerinsky who was an expert in Jewish folklore, helped with the tunes.

Dicky changed more than the form of the play. He changed its essence.

Dicky was part of the young Soviet theater of the thirties. The Russian theater in the early years of the Soviet regime aspired to be sharp and innovative. Those were the days when Vakhtangov staged *Princess Tourandot* in the style of the comedia dell'arte, Meyerhold directed Mayakosky's *Mysteria Bouffa* as a political satire performed by street clowns, and Sergey Eisenstein turned the stage of the Proletkult Theater into a circus.[18]

The Soviet theater was high with what the shrewd judge Ezdak called in Brecht's *The Caucasian Chalk Circle* the short happy interlude between changing regimes. The theater was harsh. The colors were stark. The directors turned to popular theatrical genres in a revolt against the pre-revolutionary bourgeois theater that concentrated both in its repertoire (Chekhov, Gogol) and his directing (Stanislavsky) on the narrow psychological world of the individual. In the early days of the revolution there was a will to get out of the narrow scope of the individual and open up to a society that was undergoing fundamental changes. The theater looked for means of expression with wide social range. The Italian comedia dell'arte and the French farce were theatrical models from the past. The mass theater of Reinhardt[19] was the contemporary model. All three genres attracted the Soviet directors because they were non-elitist theaters, theaters that lived with the people for the people: Street theaters that performed in market places, circus tents and sport stadiums.

The revolutionary wave carried with it the Jewish theater as well. Granovsky staged "200,000" (*The Jackpot*) in the Moscow Jewish Chamber Theater, generously incorporating elements of the comedia dell'arte together with *Massezenen* [(Mass Scenes)] following the example of his mentor, the Jewish German director born in Austria, Max Reinhardt. Thus Dicky had a living example of a Sholem Aleichem play, done in a biting innovative style.

## Beyond Stanislavsky

His choice of cast tells a great deal about Dicky's interpretation. Dicky made unconventional choices of actors for the roles of Nissy the janitor of the cold synagogue, and Feiga Lea his wife. The two characters which were added by Berkowitz and did not appear in the original play, were taken from other works by Sholem Aleichem. Dicky assigned male actors to both roles. Ben-Hayim, a short skinny actor played the role of Nissy while the tall robust Meskin played the role of his wife. The assignment of a male actor to play a woman heightened the comic element of the play.

Dicky liberated the play as well as the actors from psychological conventions. Although the Habima actors were educated by Stanislavsky who taught that the actor should use his inner self in order to create a role, with Dicky they indulged in a non psychological, playful kind of theater. In the words of the Habima actor Shmuel Rodensky :

"Often we build the role from within. This is our approach as the disciples of Stanislavsky. But there is no sin in finding the role from the outside, from the external details, the dress. For example, a role sometimes just does not work and suddenly something external, a hat or a walking cane gives you an insight. This happened with [the actor] Meskin in *The Treasure*. Dicky who came to direct *The Treasure* had an idea that the janitor's wife should be a male actor, Meskin, and her husband the tiny Ben-Hayim. In those days they used to work on a play for six months. They were great friends, that is Dicky and Meskin, they used to drink together, but when it came to do the part, Meskin was horrible. One day Dicky said to Meskin: 'Aaron, it does not work.' He went to the artistic board and said: 'Gentlemen, I had a beautiful idea, but it didn't materialize. I therefore ask you to find a replacement for Meskin.'

However they were friends, so when the costumes arrived Dicky asked Meskin to carry on with the role. Meskin went into his dressing room; they put the wig on his head, he put on a kerchief, they gave him big breasts, he looked in the mirror, began shrugging his shoulders and giggling like a woman. Suddenly he caught the role. When he came out on stage, Dicky gave a scream, it was much more than a shout: 'You got it!' His idea was there. He knew what he wanted from the actor and it worked. See, an external element gave him everything!" [20]

Dicky's idea was to visualize the relationship between the husband and his wife. The huge Feiga Lea dominated her tiny husband. As can be seen in the following scene:

"Feiga Lea (to Benny): And you must be an expert in that treasure business. They say that you have already dug one over there.

Lazer Wolf: and you came here to help, and once they dig it out you will schlep it to America and stick your tongue out at us.

Nissy: Lazer Wolf, I cannot believe that Benny would rob a town of poor people...Jews, I say...

Feiga Lea: What does it matter what you say? Let us hear what he says."[21]

The townspeople start digging and Feiga Lea brings her tiny scared husband on a pushcart.

"Nissy: (yawns)

Feiga Lea: Woman! What are you yawning for? Open your mouth to swallow the entire cemetery?

Nissy: Feiga Lea, I'm collapsing.

Feiga Lea: Woman! He wants to sleep, to sleep!"[22]

The fight between the two gains momentum and, short of hitting each other, resembles the arguments between Punch and Judy, the fighting couple of the English puppet theater. In the following sequence the usually docile husband revolts:

Nissy: Quiet...Don't upset the treasure.

Feiga Lea: Nissy, don't get excited, lie down.

"Nissy: Why should I lie down? Who is asking you what to do? Red cow! Big ox. Damn you! Damn you!"[23]

The farcical style blew the comic elements in the characters up to giant proportions. To this end Dicky exaggerated the costumes, using huge felt beards, heavily made up faces, and clothing made of rags. He also used stark vocal contrasts. The actor Finkel had a thundering bass voice in the role of Lazer Wolf, and the actor Meskin had a shrill falsetto in the role of Feiga Lea.

### Yidl the Money Lender and His Son Itsik

The tragic hero is always lonely. He may be surrounded by people, but an invisible wall cuts him off from the rest of the world. Comic heroes come in pairs; Gargantua and Pantagruel, Don Quixote and Sancho Panza, Laurel and Hardy. A tragedy can happen to one man on a solitary rock as it does to Prometheus. Comedy thrives on multiplicity. *Midsummer Night's Dream* ends with four marriages.

In *The Treasure* we find yet another comic pair, Yidl, the money lender and his son Itsik. Hanale Händler played the part of Itsik in the 1928 production tells about her work under Dicky:

"Yidl and even more so his son Itsik, were filthy and smeared with dirt. The child was all in rags, in fact he did not walk, but rather crawled on the stage like a dog, and his father led him on a leash. Yidl beats Itsik all the time, and makes sure that he does not escape. Yidl hopes to find the treasure through his son, who supposedly knows where it is hidden. He ties him and beats him up so that he will not escape. When he comes to visit the house of his future bride Esther, that is the house of Levy Mozgovyer, he is in constant fear that Benny, the shrewd American, will steal the child from him. That is why during the conversation between them, Yidl pushes the child under the cloth covered table. The child loses patience during the long conversation and from time to time his head or his little legs peek out from under the table. His father kicks him back under as the conversation continues on in an ostensibly calm, businesslike manner."[25]

Dicky used all the tricks of his trade to make the farce complete. This included the physical comedy of the circus. Itsik had a running nose that he wiped on the dirty sleeves of his shirt. The *Melamed* (teacher), would come up to him from time to time with a huge dirty handkerchief and wipe his nose. This was always accompanied by a tremendous sound.

Dicky instructed Händler who played the child never to stop crying. Itsik howled so violently that the dialogue on stage could hardly be heard.

Another circus-like element was the appearance of the child on a goat. In Palestine the troupe performed in the Jewish settlements and had no trouble finding some skinny little goat for each performance. In Berlin, the impresario asked the zoo for a goat. The German goat however was completely different from the Jewish one. It was so tall that Hanale Händler could hardly mount it. It was well taken care of, had sleek snow white fur, and had nothing of the comic misery of the Jewish goat about it.

The farce reaches its peak when the townspeople try to get precious information about the whereabouts of the treasure from the child. The child does not understand why suddenly everybody is interested in him. Frightened, he runs away and climbs up on a huge ladder to get as far as he can from them.

The Jews gather at the foot of the ladder, but since they lack the agility of the child and cannot climb after him, they try to make him come down by all kinds of odd means. They make faces, offer him sweets and candies, and threaten him all at the same time. In a circus like scene, the child tumbles and falls from the top of the ladder into the outstretched arms of the townspeople. The effort to make him talk renews with doubled energy. Itsik sits in the center of the stage, and the entire community gathers in a circle around him. Grown up Jews crawl on fours in an attempt to amuse the child and make him break his silence. They move around gesticulating like monkeys, barking like dogs, doing anything to please the child and make him tell his secret. They try to seduce the child with goodies. They hand him a carrot and wait eagerly for him to open his mouth, Itsik sits and eats the carrot serenely. The community is on the edge of hysterical despair. The child holds the carrot in his hand, eats it diligently with his head bent, his eyes glued to the floor, paying no attention to the antics of the townspeople who surround him. The image was so strong that some people refused to see it as a loose farce and accused the Russian director of plain anti-semitism.

A lot has been written about the contribution of the Jews to world theater. The contribution of Gentiles to the Jewish theater is less known. In fact it was an Armenian, Vakhtangov, who shaped the national Hebrew theater Habima. Dicky was therefore not the first non Jewish director of the troupe. Was he anti-semitic? The actor Klatchkin who worked under him thinks that Dicky was less biting in this satire on Jewish life than Vakhtangov was in *The Dybbuk*. Furthermore, explains Klatchkin, Dicky made the actors work, and often got his ideas from them.[26] He made them do many improvisations. Dicky did not try to ridicule the characters, but rather to stylize them. Dicky would explain his interpretation of the role to the actor and then ask him to improvise on it. Using the material

of the improvisation Dicky would build the character together with the actor. Klatchkin felt that the production had the spirit of the comedia dell'arte; highly stylized, comic characters, a lot of good natured mockery but no wickedness or malice. The characters were caricatures in the style of the comedia dell'arte; they were silly (Zelda the maid), pompous, (Mozgovyer), proud, (Benny), but never basically evil. In spite of their obvious faults, they also had a charming, hearty side. In Klatchkin's words:
"Everything was well rounded."[27]

## Filling the Stage Space

The Habima actors had to constantly move over the entire space of the stage. The stage design was characteristic of the young Soviet theater in that it was not naturalistic but economical and functional. The stage design served to propel the movement over the acting space through the use of bridges, ladders, ropes and the like.

Dicky used masks as well. When the townspeople were looking for Itsik in the cemetery, Dicky filled the space with masks. The actors both wore and held masks on rods. This filled and multiplied the carnival like commotion on the stage.

Dicky was both cautious and daring. He intensified the comic impact of the play to the maximum, sharpened the social criticism, and accelerated the pace of the performance. At the same time he was careful in his handling of the characters. Sholem Aleichem found in him a director who did not try to give the play a new meaning, but rather a new dynamic form.

The Sholem Aleichem characters found themselves in a frame that made them come out in all their vitality. In Dicky was found the long longed for synthesis between the Sholem Aleichem text and its modern theatrical expression. *The Treasure* by Dicky was a powerful combination of the Sholem Aleichem charm with the sweeping energy of the young Soviet theater.

## *The Treasure* in the Jewish Polish State Theater in 1969

*The Treasure* was performed in the Jewish Polish State Theater twice: in 1947 and in 1969. The actors-directors of the 1947 production Moyshe Szwejlich and Chewel Buzgan wrote the adaptation of the play. Their intent was not only to depict a picture of Jewish life in the past but also to find the economic causes that led to that way of life. The adaptors wrote:

"We approach Sholem Aleichem's realism with criticism. We look with modern eyes at the plot and content of the play. Looking for the reasons that brought about the situation, and the social relations at that time." [28]

The adaptors added elements of social criticism to the play. Thus they put in the mouth of Zelda, the maid, a proletarian song. The song was taken from another maid in another Sholem Aleichem sketch entitled: *Mazel Tov*:

"Bitter is the food
That gets burnt
Bitter is it to work
Beyond your strength

Bitter is the food
That has no taste
Bitter is to service
Such a madam."[29]

The question is whether these lines fit into *The Treasure*. The sketch *Mazel Tov*, written in 1889, focused on the conflict between downstairs and upstairs. The confrontation is between the rich who spend their time in leisure and hollow entertainment, and the servants who have to labor under their yoke. The folksy song blends perfectly with the class struggle of the Sholem Aleichem characters in *Mazel Tov*. There the relationship between the cook Beyle and the landlord are limited to the social antagonism between them. The song is less relevant to Zelda, the maid, in *The Treasure*. Here she is not meant to represent the poor working girl as contrasted with the idle madam.

Zelda's function in *The Treasure* was to add local flavor to the house of Levy Mozgovyer. The director of the 1969 production Juliusz Berger explains the theatrical necessity of the character:

"Levy Mozgovyer needs Zelda as living proof of his central position in town. Yidl, the money lender, is probably ten times richer than he is but he is a stingy beast with no class. Mozgovyer leads the life of a wealthy man. The very attribute of a wealthy household is a servant or a maid. Harpagon in Molière's *The Miser* cuts his domestic staff down to one man who has to switch hats and perform the duties of a coachman, servant and cook, but even the miser cannot spare him. Molière had to keep this one servant for his legendary miser because otherwise, in the eyes of the audience, he would cease to be a stingy millionaire and become a simple madman. The wealthy man has to have a domestic just as the lover needs a loved one. This is why in "200,000," (*The Jackpot*) Shimele, the tailor turned millionaire, immediately hires two domestics. Money in the bank is not a visual fact. Shimele, the tailor, becomes rich in the eyes of the audience when he rings the bell and a servant shows up. Zelda fulfils this same role in *The Treasure*. She has to make the house of Levy Mozgovyer look wealthy, and give visual credibility to the character of Levy Mozgovyer as a high class person whom everyone consults for a piece of advice."[30]

In addition Mozgovyer's wife Sheva is a sympathetic Jewish housewife which makes the bitter protest-song seem even more out of context.

Just as Sheva Mozgovyer is not a ruthless madam, Levy Mozgovyer, her husband, is not a ruthless capitalist. Sholem Aleichem did not idealize him. In the original play Mozgovyer forces his daughter to marry the repulsive Yidl but he does it not out of simple greed but because he has a vision. He believes that this way the treasure will be found and the whole town will be saved.

Buzgan and Szwejlich did not think much of Mozgovyer's dreams. They added lines that show that his motivation was strictly mercantile:

"Mozgovyer: It means that this is a deal sealed in heaven...The treasure was discovered thanks to both of us. Our right has been confirmed from above.

Yidl-The Bag: I see you have it all planned. Mine is yours, yours is mine...But before the thing with the treasure you would not even look in my direction. You would not talk about the marriage.

Mozgovyer: What marriage?

Yidl-The Bag: Lazer Baruch the matchmaker let you know...

Mozgovyer: So that's on your mind my dear...This is what I'm saying. We become through the treasure, how should I say, related...When God wills...

Yidl-The Bag: What are you blubbering about? Talk to the point.

Mozgovyer: What are we beating around the bush for? I am a partner to your treasure, and you will become a partner to my treasure...to my Esther...We will become in-laws, and let it be in a happy hour."[31]

Buzgan and Szwejlich continued the tradition of the progressive Jewish theater between the two world wars, in the manner of the Moscow State Theater under Granovsky, and the Artef in New York under Beno Schneider which adopted a socio-critical approach to the Yiddish classics, including Sholem Aleichem's works. They had to defame the character of Levy Mozgovyer not so much because Mozgovyer himself deserved it, but because his social class did.

### Nostalgia

Parallel to what Buzgan and Szwejlich call "A Critical Approach to the Period," and the attempt to see the play through an ideological prism, a second tendency is manifested in the adaptation, a lyrical and nostalgic one. Buzgan and Szwejlich tried to bring the Jewish *shtetl* back to life. They tried to recreate on stage a Jewish world that is no more.

"One could give the play a sharp realistic interpretation (the way it was done until now). But our approach was that in order to get closer to Sholem Aleichem, we had to present the play as a mirror of Jewish life in those historical circumstances, as a memory to those towns and little towns, as a memory to those Jews who disappeared forever, who nobody will ever see again in real life. This is how we adapted and prepared the play."[32]

In Buzgan's interpretation a tendency that was common to the Yiddish theater both in the east and the west after World War II is evident: A nostalgia for a lost Jewish world.

The two attitudes collide from the very start of the play. Buzgan adds a lyrical dialogue taken from the story *Treasures*[33], in the first volume of Sholem Aleichem's autobiographical work From the Fair [(Funem Yarid)]. In the dialogue, Sholem Aleichem's childhood friend Shmulik tells fascinating tales about hidden treasures and the magic ways of getting them.

"Itsik: How did you get to know all those things that you tell me about?

Shmuel: Little fool, you have heard nothing yet. I know how to extract wine from the wall, olive oil from the ceiling.

Itsik: How do you extract wine from the wall and olive oil from the ceiling?

Shmuel: I even know how to make gold out of sand, diamonds out of coal.

Itsik: How can you do that?

Shmuel: How? Through cabbala...The Rabbi is learned in cabbala...He never sleeps...

Itsik: What does he do?

Shmuel: At night when everybody is asleep he is awake.

Itsik: And you see everything he is doing?

Shmuel: How can I see since I sleep?

Itsik: So how come you know?

Shmuel: Who doesn't...All twelve wells with mercury and gold with silver and diamonds...are open for him.

Itsik: So why doesn't he have enough to eat?

Shmuel: Because he doesn't care...If he only wanted, he would stuff a thousand Rothchilds into his pocket because he knows how to get rich, he knows where the treasure is hidden...

Itsik: Where is it hidden?

Shmuel: Nobody will dispute that there is a treasure in our shtetl..."[34]

In contrast to the enchanted lyrical atmosphere of the children's dialogue, the first act opens with a realistic picture of a depressed social and economic situation. The peddlers sing a gloomy song:

"A shopkeeper sits in his shop
The hundredth shopkeeper on the street
He sits and thinks of a buyer
Outside it is dark and humid

Suddenly a customer shows up
A customer the size of a pea
He wants a herring for a nickel
And he interrupts his train of thought

The other shopkeepers see him
The hundred shopkeepers on the street
They eat him up with their eyes
Eyes full of envy and hate"[35]

Nostalgia and social criticism alternate throughout the adaptation and leave the play without a clear direction.

## The lyrics

The play opens with a song about the hundred shopkeepers. In fact, even the prologue, in which the children tell the story about the hidden treasure ends with a song. The adaptation suffers from a premise that goes back to the inception of the Jewish theater, namely that there cannot be a Yiddish play without songs. The writer Dineson reminds us that songs were part of the Yiddish theater from the very start:

"I don't know, if Abraham Goldfaden, the father of the Yiddish theater decorated his newborn with so many songs because he followed the example of the Purim Plays such as 'The Haman Play,' 'The Selling of Joseph,' 'Saul's Reign,' and the like, which were made up solely of rimes and songs. Couldn't Goldfaden imagine a theater without rimes, a plot on the Yiddish stage without songs, or was it his deliberate intent?"[36]

The addition of songs to the play represents a problem because although charming folksongs like "The Messiah Will come" add color and flavor to the performance, the adaptors added hollow theatrical couplets as well. Thus after they mutually confess their love in simple prose, Benny and Esther declare their love in song:

"Benny: Don't say that...To die is easy. To live is much harder; to live and fight for life. Life, Esther, is a struggle, a hard one...(takes her hands) I will fight for you Esther...for you, my destiny.

In my garden dear Esther,
I discovered a beautiful flower.
Esther:
I found a savior for my suffering.
You my love came along."[37]

Certainly this is an addition that makes one move uneasily in one's chair.

## Unnecessary changes

The changes made by Mikhoels in order to make *Tevye* more acceptable to the Soviet regime might seem repulsive, however they are politically understandable.

When Dicky dressed Holoveshke in his version of *The Treasure* with ritual fringes over his Russian policeman's uniform he had a reason for it. He wanted to turn the play into a tragic farce, and used stark visual effects for the purpose. Some objected to his sharp interpretation, however everybody understood it perfectly well. Understanding some of the changes introduced by Buzgan seems much more difficult. A question to which there seems to be no answer is why Buzgan changed the characters' order of appearance. In the original play it is the dialogue between Mozgovyer and Elke, the widow, who lost her golden coin in the cemetery that causes

Benny to trick his uncle by impersonating a ghost. Mozgovyer's stubborn resistance to the convincing argument of the widow proves to Benny that reason will not work with his uncle. In Buzgan's adaptation, Elke appears after the phony ghosts scene, in contradiction to dramatic logic. Another uncalled for change is the addition by Buzgan of his own lines to the text. In the original play the ghosts order Yidl, the money lender, to marry the widow Elke. Buzgan adds a scene in which Yidl hurries to the widow's house. There he finds her daughter, Breindl. The scene has no dramatic *raison d'être* and is vulgar to boot. Here are a few lines from this awkward scene:

"Yidl-The Bag: Well well...touch wood, a beautiful girl...
Breindl: Mother says that I have enough weight for two.
Yidl-The Bag: And where will she find so much dowry?"[38]

Buzgan changed the course of the play. This had often been done before. Many theater people from Kessler, the star of the Yiddish theater in New York at the beginning of the century, to Bunim in Tel Aviv, objected to Sholem Aleichem's dramatic technique. However there has always been a unanimous consensus among theater people about the beauty of Sholem Aleichem's language. The next passage where Berkowitz describes his efforts to sell *The Treasure* to the stars of the Yiddish Theater illustrates that point:

"And Lubarsky could not withhold any longer, handed him one of his Russian cigarettes and asked him openly: So what do you have to say Mister Kessler about our Sholem Aleichem? Well yes... answered Kessler, after a short silence, in his broken language made of lots of English and a little Yiddish... Your cigarettes are excellent you know, where do you buy them?...Now, as for the play...Well yes...Let me tell you Gentlemen...It is all right...brilliant dialogues...pearls, you know...people talk...a pleasure to listen...like Mother and Father used to, you know...pearls! And the small roles...They're all right, all right!...Well made, like oil paintings you know...The poor Jewess with the golden coin...This is, believe me, a work of art...A good portrait, honestly!...And everything around it...How do you call it?...I mean the atmosphere... very... pleasant...like... like...like when you were a child...on *Shabes* you know... you know...It's all right, all right!...Yes, but...the main thing, the center...This Jew, you know...the main role...What is his name?...The guy with the brains... O yea, Mozgovyer...Gentlemen I can't understand him!...Who is he? What is he?...I mean, what's his point?...A madman? An idiot? A crook?..."[39]

This kind of an ambivalent approach to Sholem Aleichem's drama characterizes a good many people in the Jewish theater: Criticism about the dramatic craftsmanship on the one hand and on the other hand unreserved admiration for the linguistic flavor of the characters.

The actor, Dogim, wrote in the program of the performance in the Jewish Polish State Theater:

"Notwithstanding the fact that Sholem Aleichem's drama is not a model of complicated theatrical architecture, Sholem Aleichem was the most performed writer in the Jewish, and not only the Jewish theater. This is due to the fact that Sholem Aleichem's word pictures are always dynamic, eventful and rhythmic. The best dramatic scenes in Sholem Aleichem's work are often based not on the action, but on the words, on the verbal action rather than on the situation - the reason why it was easy to stage many of Sholem Aleichem's works that were not written as a play."[40]

It is therefore very surprising to find changes in the language of the characters in Buzgan's adaptation. For instance Buzgan added a repetitive phrase ("Hard luck to my middle years") to the outbursts of Elke the widow. An endless repetition of a phrase does not transform a tasteless sentence into a folksy expression. It is hard to understand why Buzgan and Szweilich his collaborator, thought it fit to improve the language of Sholem Aleichem.

### Juliusz Berger directs *The Treasure*

Juliusz Berger directed the revival of *The Treasure* in the Polish Jewish State Theater in 1969. He used the Szwejlich-Buzgan adaptation from 1949, but gave it a more lyrical interpretation. The key to Berger's interpretation lies in his analysis of the collective dream of the treasure. The dream about the treasure was not a dream about becoming rich - explains Berger.

"The desire for money in Sholem Aleichem is completely different that in Ben Johnson or Molière. The lust for money is not selfish like that of Volpone or Harpagon. The money, the treasure, is the only means that enables the Jew in the diaspora to have a dignified life. The money is for the Jew, part of a bigger dream. A dream about escape from life of misery and uncertainty. This is why, the motif of the treasure is in its Jewish version a fantastic and romantic one."[41]

Berger finds that the romantic figure in Sholem Aleichem's comedies is not the young man (Benny, Motl) who desires to marry the young woman (Esther, Beylke), but the visionaries and the dreamers (Levi Mozgovyer, Shimele Saroker) that come on the stage with enthusiasm and a candid belief in a treasure. In Berger's words:

"First and foremost you have here the finest and the best in Sholem Aleichem's work - the dream. This is the Jewish romanticism. This is a different kind of romanticism. What could a Jew dream about in those days? The dream of an independent Jewish State was for him then an abstract thing. The only dream he could have was about independence. To be independent, that is to have the means, that is to have the money. Independence, taking in consideration the concepts of that time was money. The only means to achieve independence, was to achieve financial independence. That is to have so much money that you could buy off anyone and anything. This is the idea. It is not a cynical one. Interestingly enough, it is a romantic one. Somehow, every play about money, take Molière's *The Miser*, is a play about some cynical crippled degenerated type of a person...The economic circumstances created such a type, the miser. He understands that money gives power...The Jew does not look for that kind of power. The miser needs money, because he knows that under those circumstances, money gives power. Power! The Jew does not look for power. The exact opposite of the common belief among gentiles. The Jew wanted the money in order to achieve independence. A national autonomy. He would be able this way to survive as an individual and as a nation. This is Sholem Aleichem's dream. To live with dignity. It wouldn't be enough to be like the others - this is too little. The dream is to live better, more humanly than the others. For Mozgovyer the money is the means not the end. A treasure, in another play, it is a big win, in another story it is the stock market, or an inheritance. An inheritance, a treasure, a big win, a big profit, the motif is an eternal one. It is a universal motif. In Yiddish literature it is the same motif, yet different. In Ben Johnson's *Volpone*, in the works of Shakespeare, what is at stake is to get on top of the others, to soar above the average. There the money is the end. In Sholem Aleichem the money is the means. It is a way to live fully, creep out of the ghetto, and become a person."[42]

Berger's philosophical concept had dramatic implications. The little town, the *shtetl*, had to be shown with all its poverty and misery because if we see more or less normal shopkeepers, the dream about the treasure becomes a lust for money. Those people are poverty stricken. This is why he chose to present the shops as dog houses. The treasure is the dream of poverty. Only if it is presented as such will the poetic angle come out. Berger explained:

"Those are little shopkeepers. Those are tiny shops, and Buzgan added a song that they all sing...'A shopkeeper sits in his shop, the hundredth shopkeeper in town, etc.' This somehow fits the atmosphere of the *shtetl*. Sholem Aleichem places his plays and stories in different locations. You have little towns, towns, and even big cities, like Kiev. *The Bloody Joke* takes place in Kiev. But this is a little town, tiny little town. The size of a sigh".[43]

## A Lyrical Approach to the Text – Berger's Esther

The sympathy Berger had for the dream of the treasure made his approach completely different from that of Dicky in the Habima production of 1928. Berger did not ridicule or distort the characters to grotesque dimensions. In Dicky's production Esther was stupid and aggressive. Michael Ohad wrote about her:

"I will never forget how Fanny Lubitsh went berserk in the role of the daughter, Esther in Dicky's production: 'Whom must I marry? This chick?' she would say and point to Hanale Händler who played the role of Itsik, as she always played the urchins in Habima. The townspeople calmed her down 'No, little Esther, with this rooster' - and they would point to Yehoshua Bertonov, who played brilliantly, although obviously reluctantly his most unsympathetic role, that of Yidl the money lender."[44]

Berger remained faithful to the Sholem Aleichem romantic concept of the Jewish daughter.

"I somehow imagine Esther to be somewhat educated, she can read Russian, in other words she is one of the typical Sholem Aleichem's girls. (Tevye's daughter reads Russian in a village!) I think that Sholem Aleichem had a special feeling for young women. If you look at the women in his works such as *Sender Blank* or *Hard to Be a Jew* you find a certain analogy. The first is a big city girl, the other a provincial one, but they have things in common. First they are beautiful. Esther has to be beautiful because otherwise she would not be a treasure Mozgovoyer and Yidl trade. 'You will give me my treasure. I will give you my treasure.' Then she comes from a fine, respectable family. She is Mozgovyer's daughter. She has two things going for her, her family tree and her beauty. Jews have always put a high value on beauty. She is a naive girl, but in a romantic way. What do I mean by that? Very lyrical, helpless, childish even, because this is a young girl. In those days girls were married off very young at the age of fifteen, sixteen. She must be fifteen or sixteen. Sholem Aleichem wrote nineteen. He was in a way moralistic. Take his story of Tseitl [In *Tevye The Dairyman*]. Tseitl is not even eighteen, if my memory does not fail me. Those are young kids. My mother married at the age of sixteen. At seventeen she already had a child. This is why I am saying that Esther must be very young and helpless. A lyrical, a romantic figure."[45]

## Levy Mozgovyer

Berger did not have an ideological concept which determined the interpretation to the play. He did not divide the characters into categories according to their social class as did the soviet director,

Granovsky. There were no stereotypes. The task of the director was to understand the character. This is how he grasped Levy Mozgovyer:

"They are such a respectable family. Everybody wants to be admitted into their circle although he is a merchant just like the others...Yidl is fifty times richer than he is, but Yidl is a crook, a stingy dog, a shit eater. He would lie and sleep on the money, and never enjoy it. Mozgovyer is a wealthy Jew. He lives a decent life. He has a maid. His daughter is beautifully dressed in European style. The wife also. You can say that they are in a way somewhat emancipated. He is an observant Jew, but he is not a reactionary."[46]

Besides being the director Berger also played the role of Levi Mozgovyer.

"I played him as the king among them, the Jews are crippled, tiny people. Levi Mozgovoyer is the aristocrat. So to speak."[47]

Berger believes that Sholem Aleichem did not wish to present Levi Mozgovyer as a tyrannical father in the vein of Molière's or Goldfaden's comedy. We have to keep in mind, says Berger, that in the culture of the 19th century, there was nothing wrong with marrying a young daughter off to an old wealthy widower:

"This is not negative. A human being is no more than a human being. Mozgovyer wants to have a part in the treasure. He has only one way to do it, that is to marry off his daughter to Yidl the money lender. In those days giving a daughter to an old rich man was no sin. It was a common thing. Every parent wished that his daughter will not marry some penniless young man but rather an old man with a lot of money. A widower. The best thing was a widower. The famous dream in Sholem Aleichem's *Tevye* bears this out:

Lazer Wolf is a widower, a butcher, and Golde is willing to give him her daughter right away. A fine young daughter. So Tevye has to make up a dream to dissuade Golde from the match. Levy Mozgovyer's behavior is quite ordinary. In those days love, shmove, who took love into consideration?"[48]

The characters in Berger's interpretation were not unidimensional. Levy Mozgovyer is not made of one piece in the way Harpagon is a miser. He is much more heterogenous. All year long he is a merchant with a practical mind. Yet, the treasure mania caught up with him. Levi Mozgovyer in Berger's interpretation is a realist and a dreamer in the same time.

"You can find Jews like that. There is a businessman, a bandit, a gangster in Vienna. He has fifteen shops. If you go to him to buy something, he will cheat you...And the same Jew writes poems and plays. When he meets an actor he says: 'You have to listen to this.' He sits down and reads. Now how can you reconcile the two things? On the one hand he is a loan shark, a terrible character, and on the other hand he writes poems and plays."[49]

## Benny

According to Berger, what mattered most to Sholem Aleichem about his characters was their vitality. The Sholem Aleichem characters drew their vitality from Jewish life. Benny is removed from it. This explains the weakness of Benny's character.

"Benny is a nice guy, he works, he has a farm, he is an emancipated guy, but we European Jews do not see him as one of us. He has a different mentality, a different way of thinking, a different cultural background, something else altogether. Not ours, not folksy. From this point of view, there is a doubt whether he is Jewish at all, because looking through Sholem Aleichem's eyes, the Americans are not Jews. Israelis would not be Jews for him either. He would not have anything to write about them because he would not be able to discern their specificity. That which was a stigma in the eyes of those who lived with the Jews, the Christians, the peasants, that which was a flaw in their eyes, was for Sholem Aleichem a fantastic asset, the particularity of the Jews. Eastern European Jews were different, different from the Russians, from the Poles, from the Ukrainians.

Question: And Benny is in first and foremost an American?
Answer: He is an American."[50]

## Holoveshke

Holoveshke illustrates perfectly the Bergsonian idea of comedy. He is a mixture of completely alien elements. A Russian officer who was a *shtetl* Jew, a representative of the imperial power who would bend the law for a plate of gefilte fish. His speech is a mixture of Yiddishized Russian and Russified Yiddish. Still, Berger wanted to portray this character with psychological complexity rather than as a stock character.

"Holovoshke should be played as a human being...Sholem Aleichem drew a sketch of the character. A complex and rich character. If you play him properly, with talent, everything will come out. You will see the convert and the Jew. You will see an unhappy man who falls in love with a beautiful girl and cannot marry her."[51]

Comedy is in a way a tougher genre than tragedy. It offers no sympathy for its heroes. On the contrary, it invites the audience to laugh at their mishaps. Berger wanted a softer, more lyrical approach to the text. *The Treasure*, a comedy, borders in his interpretation on psychological drama.

## *The Treasure* and the Critics

The performance at the Hebrew national theater Habima was an outstanding success. The critic of the Davar wrote:

"The premiere of the tragic-farce in three acts, *The Treasure*, by Berkowitz based on Sholem Aleichem, played successfully to a full house in the expo-auditorium in Tel Aviv, and received the warmest response probably ever seen on the Israeli stage."[52]

However this same critic also regretted the fact that the performance was:

"exaggerated in its tone and loud."[53]

The director overused theatrical effects such as masks, and in addition some scenes were too long. However, on the whole, the final artistic balance was positive.

"The new production of Habima can be seen as a great theatrical triumph."[54]

Among the positive qualities were: brilliant comic interpretations by Gnesin (Holoveshke) and Meskin (Feiga Lea), and convincing acting by Bertonov (Yidl the lender). The visual effects were often impressive, and the wedding that concluded the play were comic and full of life. The success was due to the director and actors alone, since the play was in his words:

"poor in its literary and human content."[55]

The national poet Bialik who followed the work of Habima closely, congratulated the director Dicky after the show. The critic quoted Bialik who mentioned the fact that this Jewish theatrical masterpiece was the work of a gentile, the Russian Dicky.

"We never refrained from calling on the gentiles to teach us art. Our temple was built by a Phoenician."[56]

The critic of the daily <u>Haaretz</u> was also full of praise for the performance, especially the excellent team work which brought the entire *shtetl* to the stage as a collective character who mesmerized the public:

"This is one of the most accomplished performances in Habima, wonderful team work. The details complement each other. There are not many big roles, but each role is well made, and though heterogenous, they blend into a single gallery of portraits."[57]

The critic thought that although the director did not give a realistic picture of the *shtetl*, he did give an authentic one.

The critics in the Jewish press in Europe were on the whole positive about the performance of *The Treasure* in Habima. The reservations were of an ideological rather that theatrical nature. The critically negative attitude towards the diaspora, inherent in the play, provoked anger. Hillel Zeitlin protested in an article entitled "No, this is not us, and these are not our parents:"

"My intention is not to analyze the acting from a purely artistic point of view. I leave it to the quote unquote professional critics. Since they were so enthused about the performance of *The Treasure*, they must know why...I only wish to give my personal impressions of the thing and the way the thing was played. Had I not known

Jews, or say I had known them only through the writings of Mendele or Sholem Aleichem, I would perhaps believe both the playwright and the players, that a whole *shtetl* can suddenly become fresh, joyful and crazy, look for a treasure that never existed, make fools of themselves with no exception, run around the whole time like savages who dig for treasure in the cemetery because of the blabbing of some child who found a coin and does not even know where he found it. All that was knotted into a whole tangle of matchmaking around an American 'all-rightnik' who made fun of everyone and was himself no more than a fool. Since, thank God, I happen to know Jews not from our so called classics, but from life, watching *The Treasure* in Habima I could not pay attention to all the artistic gimmicks which they showed, because everything in me was screaming 'No! This is not how we are, and this is not how our parents were.'"[58]

Unlike Zeitlin, Itskhok Kazanelson did not have any reservations concerning neither the content of the play nor its performance, which he described as a 'miracle'. Kazanelson reiterates the well-known argument about Sholem Aleichem's dramatic looseness and therefore attributes the success of the play solely to the work of the director and the actors of the Habima ensemble.

"Sholem Aleichem, albeit a great writer, was a weak playwright. The success of Dicky's *Treasure* is not his. Just as the helpless An-sky is not the cause for the success of Vakhtangov's Dybbuk. One should thank Dicky and the actors of Habima. It is their achievement, they happily carried out the difficult assignment and built a majestic castle practically in the air, without the foundation of a literary work. They are the creators of their own literary work. After The Dybbuk this is Habima's second miracle."[59]

## *The Treasure*: Epilogue

*The Treasure* in its various interpretations reflects significant stages in the short and eventful history of the Yiddish theater. In the beginning there was Sholem Aleichem's pioneering attempt to convert the Jewish theater which presented shund plays into a theater committed to high artistic standards. The refusal of the stars in the American Yiddish theater to collaborate with him testifies to the mediocre quality of the Yiddish theater of the time.

The production of Habima in 1928 is too, a faithful reflection of the state of the Jewish theater of the time. The production echoes the rebellious spirit of Soviet Jewish theater in the aftermath of the Russian revolution.

The productions of the Polish Jewish State Theater is typical of the contemporary Jewish theater - the Sholem Aleichem text is shrouded in nostalgia for a lost Jewish world.

## 5. Tevye The Dairyman

In spite of the hardships in putting *Stempenyu* on stage in 1907, Sholem Aleichem believed that the Yiddish theater was capable of reaching artistic heights. He had faith in the talent of the actors of the Yiddish stage.

Apparently the very impulse to adapt the *Tevye1* monologues to drama came from the Jewish theater. The idea was simple. Since *Tevye* was made out of several monologues built around one person, Tevye, it lent itself to dramatic adaptation centered around one super role, the very thing the stars of the Yiddish theater were looking for. Sholem Aleichem even had specific actors in mind. The Jewish German actor, Schildkraut, or the American Jewish actor, Jacob Adler. From his place of residence in Switzerland he wrote to Dovid Pinsky in February of 1914:

"It's a pity, they tell me, that I didn't use the type [Tevye] for the stage. He would create for a good actor a giant role and win fame for his writer. Those words got into my nose, and years ago, when I read the critics about Schildkraut's appearance in the Jewish theater, I felt like transforming *Tevye* into a play for the great Schildkraut, but by the time I finished the play, I had already read about the failure of the great actor, due to his real or affected hoarseness and I kept my play hidden away in the drawer. This winter I went back to my *Tevye*. I recalled that in America there was another great artist, Mr. Jacob P. Adler, although a hard man to do business with, but truly an artist, and I realized that *Tevye* was made for him. I rewrote the play again and again and again, the way I always do, and now it is ready to the nth degree."[1]

Sholem Aleichem adjusted to the demands of the Jewish theater, and shaped a play built around one central axis, one super-role, that challenged and flattered the ego of the people who mattered in the Yiddish theater: The stars.

Sholem Aleichem was willing to accommodate the needs of the commercial theater, but without degrading the artistic level of his play. The play was free of cheap theatrical ingredients such as stereotypical characters, off-color jokes and catchy lyrics. Two elements remained: The text and the acting. A challenge faced both playwright and actor: They had to fill the stage with their talents alone. Sholem Aleichem thought he was ripe for the challenge, and he looked for an ally among the actors. In the letter to the playwright Dovid Pinsky he wrote further:

"No astounding effects, burlesque jokes, patriotic songs, dead children and the like, are to be found in the play. However the play contains both tragic and comic situations, jokes, songs, breathtaking scenes, and singing, but the main thing is that from the first act to the last curtain, Tevye pulls out all the stops, the audience laughs and gets to love him more and more, and if someone like Adler will play it, the role will become his crowning glory and will make him the darling of the public in his older years. Golde too (Mrs. Adler) would have almost as big a role, from beginning to end, as three or four strong roles for three or four daughters. In short it's 'alright' all around. There are even things to do for a comedian but only in one act. There is however enough of the comic in Tevye himself, interwoven with touching tragedy and a language that no actor has even dreamt about. The language of Tevye, with his self invented Talmudic commentaries and his tampered proverbs."[2]

In his attempt to present *Tevye* on the Jewish stage Sholem Aleichem was ahead of his time. *Tevye* became, just as Sholem Aleichem predicted "a grand role in the hands of a great actor." It did bring fame to both writer and performer, but this happened when Maurice Schwartz put on the play for the first time, in 1919, three years after Sholem Aleichem's death. The play has remained a classic of the Jewish stage to this day.

## The Various Versions of the Play

The monologues of Tevye were written by Sholem Aleichem in different periods and not as parts of one preconceived work. However, over the years Sholem Aleichem came to consider the separate monologues as chapters of one novel. A novel wherein Tevye is repeatedly confronted with the choices his daughters make, choices that go against his conservative view of the world. The story of Hava, the daughter who marries a non Jew and converts, is the most dramatic in the novel. When Sholem Aleichem started to work on the dramatic adaptation of Tevye in 1913, with the Beilis blood trial and the expulsion of the Jews from the villages in the background, he chose the episode of Hava as the central axis of the play. The drama, unlike the novel has a happy end. Hava returns to her family and her people.

Sholem Aleichem wrote a few versions of the play before coming up with the final, authorized and published version. In my research for this book I came across three versions of the play. All three manuscripts are kept in "Bet Sholem Aleichem" in Tel Aviv. The richest in romantic conflicts is the version which we will refer to as version A. Khone Shmeruk writes about version A:

"In 'Bet Shalom Aleichem' in Tel Aviv is kept a manuscript of a drama without title, that is by all indications one of the versions of 'Tevye's Daughters' about which Sholem Aleichem corresponded with the famous actor Jacob Adler and the writer Dovid Pinsky in January and the beginning of February 1914...Already the manuscript of 'Tevye's Daughters' shows only one substantial difference to the content of the monologues, and this is the dénouement of Hava's affair with the Ukrainian husband. The fourth act takes place in Yehupits in the rich house of Hava's sister Beylke and her husband. Hava shows up in her sister's house, after she has left her husband. The dialogue between the two sisters tells us why. Hava says that her Ukrainian husband...'has the guts to throw in my face that my father will not stop at anything, to get at least some drops of their holy blood for the passover matzos.' Reacting to such accusations Hava leaves him, and comes back to Beylke, in order to make up with her family and travel 'far, far' out of Russia, so that she can return to her Judaism, since in Russia such a step would be impossible. (pp. 133-134 of the manuscript) Towards the end of the play Tevye and his wife show up in Beylke's house, and after he hears what has happened to Hava, Tevye gives in to the supplication of Beylke and Golde, hugs Hava and takes her back to the family and her people."[3]

Shmeruk, who went through Sholem Aleichem's correspondence, noticed that version A did not satisfy the writer. In fact, an examination of the two other versions of the play shows a noticeable improvement. We shall first look at an incomplete version, that we shall call version B.

## Version B

The manuscript contains only the last act. The *dramatis personae* include Tevye, Beylke, and her husband Padhotsur.

As in Version A, the last act also takes place in the luxurious home of Beylke and her wealthy husband.

Version B is superior in dramatic technique and in the complexity of the characters. In Version A, Padhotsur is involved in the plot, but in a clumsy undramatic way. The scene takes place in his house, the characters speak about him, but he himself is absent. In Version B, Padhotsur appears on stage as an exuberant *nouveau riche* in all his theatricality. He wears a tuxedo and patent leather shoes, smokes a cigar, and speaks an assimilated Russified Yiddish. In opposition to the snobbish empty character of Padhotsur, Beylke is quiet and endearing. The sympathetic portrayal of Beylke is the major change from Version A, in which Beylke adopts the characteristics of her husband and seemed to enjoy her position as the self-indulging bourgeois wife. This was hardly compatible with the representation of young Jewish women in Sholem Aleichem's writing in general, and in Tevye in particular. Sholem Aleichem portrays them as sensitive, bright, and sincere.

Version B deals mainly with Beylke and her husband, Padhotsur. The main issue in this version is Padhotsur's attempts to rewrite his genealogical tree. He wants to send Tevye to Palestine so that people will say that his father-in-law is living in the Holy Land rather than selling dairy products from a horse-drawn wagon.

## Version C

The problem of Padhotsur is actually marginal to the entire set of the Tevye stories. This is probably why Sholem Aleichem abandoned Version B and wrote a third Version, concentrating on Hava and her conversion in the context of the expulsion of the Jews from the villages.

The manuscript of the third version, Version C, is almost identical to the play as it was published after Sholem Aleichem's death. Shmeruk wrote about the difference between Version C and Version A:

"The atmosphere that prevailed during the Beilis trial, in 1913, showed how deeply rooted the belief was among the Christian population in Russia, that Jews used Christian blood in matzos. Still, the portrayal of Hava's Christian husband in *Tevye's Daughters* (Version A) is somewhat crude. Probably Sholem Aleichem himself felt he went beyond the plausible when Hava's 'progressive' husband, this 'second Gorki,' as Hava describes him in the monologue from 1906, heaps such a senseless accusation upon Tevye.

In the last version of the play Chvedor (Sholem Aleichem calls him Fedya in the final version) was accused by Hava of one thing - the fact that he didn't tell her about the impending deportation of the Jews from the village. The reader can assume that he acted this way in order not to sadden Hava and prevent her from taking drastic action. Here there is no blemish on the character of Chvedor. But as expected, Hava, a faithful daughter of Tevye, reacts in a worthy manner. She leaves her husband and the village, as if to show that the conversion did not cut her off from her family and her people. Their plight awakens in her a feeling of solidarity with them. She regrets her choice and repents for her actions. Her Christian husband figures in this only marginally."[4]

These are notable changes but the importance of version C lies elsewhere. In his last version Sholem Aleichem finally found the very core of his play. His work in the theater taught him the importance of the aristotelian unity of action. He realised that focusing on a single conflict strengthens the dramatic punch. Over the course of the three versions the play evolved from the large epic to a tight dramatic unit which focuses on one central conflict.

The essence of the conflict changed too. The nature of any society is best conveyed by the role women play in it. A change in society is therefore best portrayed by the change women experience in it. In the first two versions Sholem Aleichem devotes much of his attention to the portrayals of the sons-in-law. In the last version he concentrates on Tevye's daughter: Hava. Sholem Aleichem shifted his focus from the men in his tentative drafts, to Hava, as the play crystallized. Sholem Aleichem fully understood the magnitude of the change brought about by the modern age in Jewish society. A woman was best suited to represent this change on stage.

## The Berkowitz Adaptation and the Production in the Hebrew national theater Habima

Berkowitz adapted *Tevye* for Maurice Schwartz and his Yiddish Art Theater [Yidisher Kunst Teater].[5] The Hebrew version is a translation of that adaptation. In his preface to the Hebrew edition of Sholem Aleichem's works, Berkowitz wrote about his reservations concerning the original text, and the modifications he found it necessary to make.

"When I started adapting the play, after the death of Sholem Aleichem, for the performance in Maurice Schwartz's theater, I realized that in its original form, the way it came out of the writer, it was unfit for the stage. The literary style, a wordy one, swallowed the dramatic element. The plot, and the characters were at their best, as in the Tevye stories, when they delivered their monologues. I therefore used the license given to me by Sholem Aleichem in his lifetime, when we collaborated on the adaptation of his plays, and I changed the dramatic structure of the play with materials that I took from the writer himself. I added to the *dramatis personae* the Russian Orthodox priest, Father Alexey, who was not a character in the play, and who was only hinted at in Tevye's monologue, in the first act, and I made him one of the major causes in the course of the dramatic events."[6]

In Sholem Aleichem's play we learn about the confrontation between Tevye and the priest as Tevye retells it in his monologue. In Berkowitz's, we see it. Tevye and the priest face each other in a build-up of dramatic scenes. Avraham Ninio, who was the assistant director in the national theater's Habima production in 1943, agreed with Berkowitz and maintained that theatrically speaking, it was more effective to see the priest on stage rather than to hear about him from Tevye. The original version is more restrained, but this very restraint diminishes the dramatic interest.

"Question: Does the fact that the priest is on stage make the play more dramatic?
Answer: Certainly.
Question: The original had perhaps more restraint, more 'decorum'...
Answer: 'Bobe Mayses'... (Nonsense)
Question: You say that there should be blood on the stage?
Answer: You doubt it? Of course."[7]

Berkowitz went beyond changing the dramatic structure. In his adaptation he also changed the spirit of the play. The confrontation between the Jewish and the Gentile world becomes simplistic and irreversible. In the original play, the love between Hava and Fedya dies because of the social and political circumstances of the time. Sholem Aleichem did not suggest any internal friction between the two lovers. Berkowitz turns Fedya into an anti-semite. In their very first lovers' quarrel in Tevye's front yard, Berkowitz's Fedya defies Hava:

"Your heart belongs to others, to your father, to your family, to your Jews...(gives her his hand) Goodbye, Yeva."[8]

Another line that Berkowitz gave to Fedya to show his anti-semitic character, appears in an episode that Berkowitz added to the scene of the deportation of the Jews from the village. Hava finds refuge in her father's house and Fedya tries to talk her into returning to him.

"Fedya: I don't understand. Where are you going to? What does it mean?

Hava: The *Zhidovka* [pejorative term for Jewess] goes with the rest of the *Zhids* [pejorative term for Jews].

Fedya: Yeva, you know very well that I...I'm not to blame...You started. You nagged me with complaints, so I lost my temper..."[9]

Avraham Ninio, Chemerinsky's assistant, who also played the part of Shloymele, Tevye's grandson, in the Habima production of 1943, explained that Berkowitz, together with the director Chemerinsky, gave Fedya an anti-semitic touch.

"Question: Was there any attempt to present Fedya as an anti-semite...

Ninio: Yes.

Question: Who said that he was anti-semitic, Berkowitz?

Ninio: Berkowitz said that he was anti-semitic, and Chemerinsky directed the play that way. The anti-semitic element exists in him. At least his father was anti-semitic. The root is anti-semitic".[10]

Berkowitz took the trouble to prepare written instructions for the actors.[11] Berkowitz tried to portray Fedya as a totally negative character. Sholem Aleichem described him as a peasant's son who discovered the world of Russian literature. The relationship between Fedya and Hava grew out of their common literary sensitivity. Berkowitz did not think much of this sensitivity.

"He learned from his father, Mikita, the strong arm in the village, to despise the life of labor and poverty that was the lot of illiterate peasants, and to aspire to a good, easy life. From his mother, Tekla, he inherited feelings of inferiority and the habit of self-denigration in dealing with smarter and more assertive people. During his four years of service in the army, he developed a superficial affinity for books. He shows-off using their vocabulary, and perhaps even scribbles some prose imitating Gorki, who like himself started in the lowest echelon of society and worked himself up to the top of the social ladder."[12]

The sensitivity of the character is interpreted by Berkowitz as an empty pose. Even his physical assets, like his agility, appeared to be fraudulent in Berkowitz's eyes.

"The basic ingredients of his personality: Weakness of character that makes him surrender facing reality (he goes along with the community that chases Tevye from the village, and obeys Hava when she sends him away from Tevye's house). He exhibits a sentimental emotionalism that reaches declamatory outbursts in most of his dialogues with her.

His expression: Talks moderately with a special intonation like reading from a book, apparently listening to himself. He admires and enjoys his talk. His movements are grandiose like those of the army officers who philosophize in high style. His steps are easy and agile like a big shot, not an awkward peasant. His gait is swift and dashing, and all his movements are meant to create an impression."[13]

Even his choice of Hava was not, according to Berkowitz, a pure romantic impulse, but rather derived from a negative attitude, an arrogance, a feeling of superiority towards the other girls in the village:

"Why did he choose Hava? There were many reasons. He despised the peasant girls, just like Mikita despised their fathers, and he would not look for a mate among them. He wanted a partner that would befit a person of his rank. None of the village girls could appreciate the charm of his person, and reach the pinnacle of his thoughts and fantasies. None would be able to listen to and understand his sublime speech. And here sparkled the lovely appealing figure of this young Jewish woman, Tevye's daughter. This Jew was famous and praised by the peasants of the village, including his father Mikita.

Fedya longs for her. (Maybe father Alexey, his educator and guide from childhood, made allusions about her, and served as a matchmaker). The Jews stand higher than the peasants. They almost approach the nobility both in their education and in their way of life, and it would be an honor for Mikita to marry his son to one of them. And the Jewish daughters are beautiful and delicate like the daughters of the nobility; they excite and attract the heart with a wondrous charm, a quaint enticing charm. The charm of an exotic and elevated race. This and more. There is a romantic dimension to it: To marry a beautiful Jewess, who converts for the sake of love is a heroic deed, a deed worthy to be written about in a novel. Who among the illiterate young village boys would dare do such a thing, such an extraordinary thing, change the steady pattern of life..."[14]

Berkowitz has dipped Fedya in hot tar. Rafael Klatchkin, who played Fedya, did not come out unharmed either. Not only did Berkowitz attack the character, he also attacked the actor who played him. In margins of the instructions Berkowitz noted:

"Written for R. Klatchkin, who rejected it, and did not read it in his clownish carelessness."[15]

Klatchkin refused to submit to Berkowitz's orders not because of "clownish carelessness," but because his artistic instincts told him to act differently. Interestingly, the actor Albert Cohen, who replaced Klatchkin in the role of Fedya, and who did not read Yiddish, and never read the original Sholem Aleichem text, also played the role in the spirit of the original text, ignoring Berkowitz's interpretation of the character. Albert Cohen explained that working on the role, he realized that Fedya could not be an anti-semite. This would stand in complete contradiction to the inner logic of the character and to the nature of his relationship with Hava.

"I didn't want to make him anti-semitic. If I didn't make him sympathetic, why would a girl like Hava fall in love with him? Why should she go with some shmuck? He was sympathetic...He was different. In those days a guy went and married a Jewess! Imagine somebody marrying an Arab woman here in Tel Aviv! This is a sensation! The two of them make a revolution! Revolution! He was a kind of outsider. You must find those tones in the role. Otherwise, it's nothing. Otherwise, everyday people got married to Jewish women. It was not a daily event. There was only one man like him in the village."[16]

Fedya, claimed Albert Cohen, belonged to the tragic heroes of the play.

"I played him like a *Shaygets* (a Christian boy) from the village. But charming. By no means unsympathetic or anti-semitic. Not at all. I (Fedya) was in some way a victim of the whole thing. I fell in love. I loved Hava and she loved me, and they didn't accept me in this family. This is how I felt about the part, and this is how Ninio allowed me to play it."[17]

The fact that Hava leaves him at the end of the play adds to the tragic dimension of the character. According to Albert Cohen, Fedya comes out of the whole thing broken hearted.

Like Albert Cohen who followed him, Klatchkin also did not think of Fedya as being anti-semitic. In reference to the question as to whether, in his opinion, Fedya would spit the pejorative designation *Zhidovka* in Hava's face as implied by Berkowitz's text, he answered laconically:

"I don't think that he ever said it to her."[18]

Klatchkin's Fedya was not complex. For Klatchkin, Fedya's daring choice comes more from egoism then from the nobility of his soul. In our interview Klatchkin summed up his interpretation of Fedya:

"He does as he pleases. But it's easier for him than it is for Hava or Tevye. He doesn't make a big deal out of it. He falls in love with a Jewess so he marries a Jewess. It's not that he is such a good person, but he works to get what he wants, and he gets what he wants."[19]

The example of Klatchkin and Cohen shows us that a play continued changing even after the last day of rehearsals. The play was first revised by the dramaturge, then modified by the director, and last but not least interpreted by the actors. The actors are not supposed to adapt the play, only to perform it. In reality however they give the final commentary to the play. After all, once the curtain has risen, the play is in their hands.

## Berkowitz – An Adaptation in Black and White

The Gentiles in Berkowitz's version of *Tevye* become more evil, and the Jews become tougher. Berkowitz made Hava say words of contempt in Fedya's face before leaving him:

"Hava: (in contempt) Leave me alone with your drunken villagers. You are not any better than they..."[20]

In the original Sholem Aleichem text, Hava has one, and only one complaint about Fedya - which we hear of indirectly from her dialogue with her sister Tseitl - namely that Fedya tried to hide the news of the expulsion of the Jews from her.

In Sholem Aleichem's version the peasants are indeed contaminated by anti-semitism, but they were obviously reluctant to chase Tevye from the village. The expulsion is presented rather as a decree dictated to the village by the imperial authority. In Berkowitz's version the peasants and Tevye share a mutual dislike. After the village elders tell him about the deportation decree, he screams at them:

"You are nothing but animals, wolves of the forest."[21]

Unlike Sholem Aleichem, Berkowitz made Tevye prejudiced against the Gentiles. Tevye discovers that they are stupid by their very nature. In his last words to the priest he says:

"All those years I thought of you as a clever Goy - cruel, but clever. But this time I see that the uncircumcised (nods with his head) are also unwise..."[22]

Berkowitz made the end harsher and less lyrical than the original. In the original play, Tevye, who is forced to abandon his home of many years, shows warmth and understanding towards his horse and even towards the cat that he has to leave behind. Berkowitz cut this scene with the cat altogether, although Sholem Aleichem considered it important, as he expressed in a letter to his wife:

"It is very touching when Tevye bids farewell to the naked walls, kisses them, and shows sympathy for the cat, saying that it shouldn't be left alone...For Christians (if the drama will make it to the non Jewish stage) it would be quite an embarrassment, that the Jew who is expelled by them, has pity for a cat..."[23]

The episode impressed Chemerinsky. Although it was missing from the text prepared by Berkowitz for the performance at the Habima Theater, the director Chemerinsky drew a cat in the prompt book, in order to emphasize the lyrical aspect of the farewell scene as Tevye leaves the village.

## Father Alexey

The actor Albert Cohen said that when Berkowitz lectured about the characters of the play to the actors of the Habima theater, he divided them into two categories: Good Jews and bad Gentiles.

In the case of Father Alexey it seems as if Berkowitz was not wrong. The priest is shrewd, bigoted, violent, and ruthless. Still, the actor Shmuel Rodensky who played the part of the priest succeeded in adding another dimension to the role. In Rodensky's words:

"The priest, harasses Tevye, and yet he has a weak spot for him. Tevye is one of the few people he could chat with. The peasants are all ignorant. He loves to sit on the veranda with Tevye, have tea and discuss religion. The priest is caught by Tevye's charm. However, the human factor in the relationship between the two is secondary. The priest sees himself first and foremost as the representative of the Orthodox Church, and in Tevye he sees the Jew. Therefore, the relationship between the two is not open and frank. Though he pretends to be benevolent, the priest is in fact hypocritical. The scene in which he makes Tevye and Golde rise up on their feet after they have knelt down and begged him to return Hava to them is especially poignant. He does not allow them to see their daughter. The priest's cruelty, said Rodensky, is religious. He is not necessarily an evil man, but his religious fanaticism makes him insensitive and cruel".[24]

The most important element in the priest's appearance, explained Rodensky, is his self-confidence. Rodendky used accessories which helped convey self-importance. He walked on the stage with a long rod. The rod made his walk solemn and stable. His long robe slowed down his steps and this also made him look important. Rodensky said that another external detail, the beard, helped him getting into the role of the old authoritarian clergyman. He would complacently caress his beard, sink his chin in his chest, and talk with a deep voice, that came from his belly.

## Hava

Hanale Händler and Hana Rovina alternated in the role of Hava in the Habima theater production. Hava, in Händler's interpretation, does not return to her family because she discovers that Fedya is anti-semitic as suggested by Berkowitz.

Hava, explained Hanale Händler, is a girl at the start of the play, and a woman towards its end. Within the period described in the play she becomes disillusioned with her romantic dream. The return to her people is in fact part of a general disillusionment. Actually, Hava falls in love with Fedya through a fictional character, and only as time goes by she discovers that the man she married is not a copy of the hero from the novels she dreamt about. Händler elaborated:

"We met at the well. Actually I was more fascinated by Gorki than by Fedya. I say to him: 'You look like Gorki.' He symbolized a whole new world for her. He was talking about socialism, he had a Rubashka [Russian shirt] on. After the marriage, I saw that life with Fedya was not life with Gorki. It was a plain life. And in addition, everybody around hated the Jews. They threw them out of the villages."[25]

The otherness in Fedya, said Hanale Händler, attracted Hava both physically and psychologically. In married life however the exotic element disappeared. This, together with the hostility of the environment, made Hava return.

"Hava's mistake was that she thought Fedya was someone else. He was not smart. He could not get the stars from above for her. She was much more interesting. But here perhaps physical attraction played a role. Sex. He was a handsome guy. Blond. In Bialystok, where I come from, the Gentile officers were walking around, and the Jewish girls were actually burning for them. It seems as if you always look for something else. Something that you don't find at home or in your neighborhood. Also, Fedya was romantic, and talked so beautifully. Later on she lived with him and got to know him better than during the courtship, when he came to her with a book by Gorki in his hand. In my town there were cases of girls who went to live with Gentiles because they thought this would be a whole new world. They got disappointed, regretted it, and returned. When I worked on the role, my hometown came back to my mind."[26]

The doubt, said Händler, gnaws at Hava right from the start. She played the wedding in a very sad way, as if Hava had a premonition of the bad things to come. She was not gay and she did not dance. Fedya's friends literally pulled her into the circle of the dance. In Hanale Händler's interpretation, Hava did not leave Fedya because he was a devil, but rather because he was a bore.

Händler like Klatchkin and Cohen disregarded the simplistic interpretation given by Berkowitz to the play. She did not change Berkowitz's lines. She changed the way they were delivered.

Her Hava was wiser, sadder, and more endearing.

## *Tevye* in Habima – Beyond the Text

The history of the *Tevye* productions in the Hebrew national theater Habima gives a better insight as to the way theater works.

Parallel to the original text, a second text was written by the director followed by a third text written by the actors.

It seems that the actors tacitly agreed to give a less angry, more humane interpretation to the characters.

However, in spite of the criticism one may have about his adaptation, Berkowitz succeeded in preserving much of the spirit of the original text. His adaptation is no doubt more dramatic than the original. It can be a useful tool in the hands of a director who knows its limitations, and realizes he has a louder, less refined version of the play.

Berkowitz's adaptation reveals a paradox. Sholem Aleichem allowed directors and actors to modify his text. Berkowitz in contrast, did not allow anyone to tamper with his modification of the original text. Actors were not allowed to omit or change a single word. Yet the language that he so jealously guarded, became problematic. In the forties, Berkowitz's Hebrew was already old fashioned. With the development of Hebrew, it became archaic. The old Sholem Aleichem Yiddish text kept its freshness whereas the later Hebrew adaptation by Berkowitz became antiquated.

## *Tevye* in the Moscow Jewish State Theater

In 1938, the Moscow Jewish State Theater produced *Tevye*. The adapters were Dobrushin and Oyslender. The director was Shloyme Mikhoels, who also played the role of Tevye.

*Tevye* underwent a metamorphosis in the production of the Moscow Jewish State Theater. I am not referring to the external changes such as the addition of characters and conflicts which did not exist in the original play and were drawn from the novel. The change was in the very nature of the adaptation. The good natured irony of the original *Tevye* disappeared, and pathos took its place.

The adapters eliminated any text that could imply lighthearted mockery of revolutionary values. Tevye's amused and skeptical attitude to this "whole thing called revolution, the good of the collective, the triumph of the working class"[27] disappeared.

The Communist Party did not regard Jews as a nation. In deference to the Soviet ideology, Tevye had to become less Jewish. Sentences that expressed the comical tension between Tevye's traditional Jewish outlook and the Gentile world were cut. The following passage where Tevye mocks his daughter's romantic choice was deleted:

"What then is he? The grandson of Rabbi Ashi? Rabbi Fedya, the son of Rabbi Mikita Galagan - the light of exile, such a Gentile, a fink, like his father before him, who sprang from strictly noble ancestry...The grandfather, may he rest in pieces, was a great heroic and fearful drunkard, and beat his wife three times a week, and his great-grandfather, may he also rest in pieces, sat day and night and devotedly guarded the pigs."[28]

Bergson[29] wrote that comedy is generated by mixing alien elements. The Talmud is not funny. A Ukrainian peasant is not funny. Tevye mixes alien elements. He uses Talmudic language to describe a Ukrainian peasant, and that is why he is funny.

Tevye makes us laugh because he is different. Making Tevye more like the Gentiles around him means making him less, not more interesting.

By making Tevye a revolutionary and a patriot, the adapters sterilized the text. Tevye's wit was replaced by repulsive earnestness.

### The Impact of Mikhoels

Mikhoels was both the director and the star of the show. He went along with the interpretation of the play given by the dramaturges Dobrushin and Oyslender. Mikhoels tried to add a touch of grandeur to Tevye, the man of the people. The actor, Israel Beker said about the performance.

"In Mikhoels' interpretation, the whole play stood on stilts. It is as if they forcibly lifted the play, made it more elevated. The performance was stiff. Stilts are not feet with live agility. Mikhoels aspired to reach philosophical truths in his role, but there was a very wide gap between him and the audience. Those were kind of confused artistic explorations on stage."[30]

Beker elaborated:

"The word pathetic is an understatement when applied to the acting of Mikhoels in the play. It was in total contradiction to my approach. When I see a play, I open my ears, and they stand like a policeman with a poised pistol ready to shoot any actor who acts this way. This was some kind of unreal theater, some broken down pathos."[31]

Mikhoels, in his double function as director and actor, exercised a major influence on the whole ensemble.

"With Mikhoels, the actors used an exaggerated speech pattern. It was as if they all stretched their bodies in an effort to reach to his level. This was the root of this theatrical disaster. All those years, the actors were not themselves, but tried to reach some ideal that was Mikhoels'."[32]

The original Sholem Aleichem text completely changed flavor in Mikhoels' version. The scene where Hodl tells Tevye that she is leaving him to join her husband in Siberia is a good example. Tevye compares himself to a hen who sat on goose eggs and hatched goslings. Once out of the shells, they do not pay any attention to their mother, and swim away in the water. Hodl answers him with a question.

"True. It is really a pity for the hen. But because the hen squawks, shouldn't the goslings swim?"[33]

I listened to a recording of this dialogue in the Moscow Jewish State Theater.[34] The intimate, humorous dialogue sounded heavily melodramatic. It would be hard to find a starker contrast to the original style of the Moscow Jewish State Theater as established under Granovsky's direction. Granovsky got rid both the Jewish *krekhts* [sigh] and the Russian pathos. Maybe the overacting of Mikhoels in *Tevye* came as a reaction to years of strictly orchestrated work under Granovsky. It is as if Mikhoels swung the pendulum back to its polar opposite: From daring grotesque to sentimental realism.

Mikhoels' problem was one of restraint. Since Mikhoels directed himself, he sometimes lost his sense of proportion. In Beker's words:

"In my first encounter with Mickhoels, I totally refuted his approach. Gradually I felt the urge to understand the man and his outlook. Then I learned to sort out for myself things that I later interwove in my theatrical work. It's like a painter who uses his palate and suddenly discovers a spot of color which makes the whole picture come alive. Those spots are the vital essence of the creative work. The question is what happens when you paint only with this hue..."[35]

Mikhoels' *Tevye* has to be understood in its historical and theatrical context.[36] The Soviet theater of the later thirties, aspired to majesty and pathos. Segments of the recording done by Mikhoels which today sound like sentimental forte were then the norm.

The greatest achievement of the Moscow Yiddish theater under Mikhoels was its very existence. Mikhoels kept the Jewish State Theater alive under the harsh political demands of Stalinism. It was a Yiddish theater with a Yiddish audience, with Yiddish dramaturges, scholars, and critics - an achievement seldom matched under much more favorable circumstances.

## *Tevye* in the Jewish State Theater in Warsaw, Poland

*Tevye* was performed in the Polish Jewish State Theater three times.[37] It was first directed by M. Lipman in 1947. In 1961, the play was adapted by Chevel Buzgan, who also played Tevye. The same adaptation was used again when the play was performed in 1970 under the direction of Juliusz Berger who also played the part of Tevye.

In his adaptation, Buzgan incorporated almost all of Tevye's daughters. In the original dramatic adaptation, Sholem Aleichem included only Tseitl and Hava, with Tseitl appearing only as an auxiliary character in the exposition of the plot.

Buzgan dealt with a number of dramatic conflicts and did not concentrate on a single one the way Sholem Aleichem did in his final version of the play.

The adaptation started with what seemed at first to be the conventional dramatic structure of the marriage of the daughter in the family as explained by Northrope Frye.[38] The young revolutionary Pertshik (Subject), is interested in Tevye's daughter Hodl (Object), and Tevye opposes the liaison between the young people (opposition).

Buzgan, however, did not use the triangular structure (Subject, Opposition, Object) as a steady axis for the play.

The dramatic adaptation jump-cuts to the next episode. The triangular structure that opens the play persists, but its components change. The young Ukrainian, Fedya (Subject, although not present on the stage) is interested in Hava (Object), and Tevye rejects him for religious reasons (Opposition). Buzgan did not keep Hava as the focus of the plot either: Menachem Mendel worms money out of Tevye, which he then frivolously invests and loses.

The play goes on incorporating yet another of the Tevye monologues: The story of Beylke, the youngest daughter, who marries into money.

The adaptation ends in an embarrassingly blatant political statement. Hava reads from Hodl's letter, in which she extols the revolution which will rise, like the sun, in the east.

## Many characters, little depth

Menachem Mendel makes two brusque appearances and disappears. His Don Quixotic charisma in the novel is completely lost on stage. The great loser of the adaptation is Hava. In Sholem Aleichem's play she is the focus of the plot. In Buzgan's version Hava's story is no more than one of many conflicts.

Like many actors in the Yiddish theater, Buzgan too suffered from the star syndrome, that is seeing the play as orbiting around one central body, the star. Buzgan built the play around one central character, Tevye, whom he played. One way of guaranteeing the predominance of the star is to minimize the other roles. In Buzgan's adaptation the significance of Tevye's partners is reduced. Paradoxically, however, the diminution of the supporting roles undermines the main character. When Hava is flat and inarticulate, the pain Tevye suffers over her affects us less. The weakness of the secondary characters finally takes away from the central character, Tevye, who is connected to them all.

## Juliusz Berger Directs *Tevye*

Julius Berger directed the revival of the play at the Polish Jewish State Theater in 1970. Berger felt that Tevye represents the Jewish collective super ego. He has most of the characteristics that Jews would like to see in themselves. In Berger's words:

"It doesn't mean that Tevye is ideal. He has flaws which make him more interesting. Tevye is stubborn, he is a bigot. Today we would look at the conflict between Tevye and Hava differently. But Tevye's weaknesses are so human that he wins our sympathy. Tevye loves his wife, his daughters, his horse. He is a sympathetic Jew and a sympathetic man, a working Jew, an honest Jew. A Jewish hero the way we would like to see him in literature and in life. There are extraordinary Jewish heroes, scholars, heroes the masses respect and even venerate. People are proud of them, but they are far above the masses. The common man respects them, but finds it hard to feel sympathy for them because they are too perfect. People would love to sit at one table with Tevye because he is one of them, he is not a world famous scholar like Maimonides or a fierce warrior like Bar-Kochba. He is not bigger than life. Tevye is a folk hero, a man with good qualities and flaws: A Jew one can have a drink with and share one's joy and sorrow...

You could say that another Sholem Aleichem character, Shimele Saroker, from *The Jackpot* is also such a hero. He is also a folksy type. But Shimele has too much of a confining professional flavor - he is first and foremost a tailor. Shimele is limited to a specific milieu, the fringe of the Jewish petite bourgeoisie. Tevye is not bound to a specific background. He is universal. He is bound to some loose definition of a village Jew. This is a general definition that does not put the hero in the vise of a specific occupation. Tevye enjoys the freedom of the wide open Ukrainian countryside, the woods and the fields that he crosses with his horse and wagon. In Tevye we also find the simplicity of the village man with his physical strength. These qualities appealed to the Jewish audience which was largely urban."[39]

## Tevye the Jew

Berger paraphrased an anecdote told by Mary Waife Goldberg in her book, *My Father, Sholem Aleichem.*[40] She writes about the milkman who was the inspiration for the character of Tevye. This milkman supplied Sholem Aleichem and his family with dairy products in their *Dacha*. After the purchase of the produce, Sholem Aleichem would stand and chat with the milkman, deriving special pleasure from his flowing conversation. His wife would call him to stop, because everybody was ready for lunch. Sholem Aleichem would hush her up and tell her that lunch could wait. He would point to the milkman and argue that he had to chat some more because the milkman was the entire Jewish nation comprised in one man. Berger found this anecdote illuminating.

"Tevye's Jewishness is not a philosophical matter. Tevye does not have any ideology. He is neither Orthodox nor a Zionist. Being

Jewish is for him more than that. It is a total, almost sensuous, knowledge. He does not hate the Gentiles. He simply knows that being Jewish is the core of his existence. It is an intuitive knowledge.

We have to understand the importance of being Jewish to Tevye, otherwise we will not be able to understand the tragedy that he experiences when Hava marries a Christian. Tevye is not happy about Tseitl's and Hodl's choices. Tseitl marries a poor sickly tailor. Hodl marries a revolutionary who is later exiled to Siberia, but Motl and Pertshik are Jewish. The pain those choices caused him was nothing compared to the pain Hava causes him."[41]

Hava is Tevye's tragedy, explained Berger. The world that seemed relatively understandable until her conversion challenged him suddenly with a question that he could not answer: How could a far fetched notion such as romantic love overcome, destroy, and annihilate what he felt was the essence of life: Judaism.

The break up in Jewish society was even more dramatic than Berger realized. Tevye and Golde are the last representatives of a millenary Jewish tradition. Hava represents the first generation of emancipated Jews. The fact that the new revolutionary generation is represented by a girl emphasizes the magnitude of the change: A patriarchal society is challenged by a woman.

The conflict at the heart of the play is a struggle between the old and the new world. Sholem Aleichem showed the break up of Jewish life in Eastern Europe at the turn of the century. *Tevye* was his literary vehicle. Jewish society was carried away by the landslide of economic and cultural changes of the time. Sholem Aleichem observed the infiltration of Russian culture into Jewish homes, down to the home of this village Jew, Tevye. Sholem Aleichem described the painting of Count Tolstoy which finds its way to the wall in Tevye's house. He described Hava, pressing Gorki's books against her heart, and the conversion that lurked, like a hidden curve at the end of that road.

The text used by the Jewish Polish State Theater is a poor one. Buzgan was a good actor but a bad dramaturge. Berger made up for the shortcomings of the text by his understanding of Sholem

Aleichem, and his charisma as an actor. He managed to bring back to the performance the depth of the original Sholem Aleichem drama.

## *Tevye* In The Cinema

In 1914, two years before his death, Sholem Aleichem wrote two scripts (in Russian) for the silent movies, *Tevye the Eternal Optimist* and *Hava - Tevye's Daughter*. The main character in both scripts was Tevye. In the film scripts Sholem Aleichem joyfully explored the possibilities offered by the new medium. The two scripts were never filmed.

## Tevye the Eternal Optimist

The script is based on Tevye's monologue *The Big Win*.[42] In the opening sequence Tevye is riding with his horse and wagon. He tries to forget his hunger in flights of fancy about a treasure that he finds lying in the middle of the road. Sholem Aleichem used the possibilities of visualization offered by the new medium, and incorporated a sequence describing Tevye's daydream:

"Tevye suddenly notices a huge bag lying in the middle of the road. He stops and approaches the bag, bends over it, unties it, and recoils in fear. In the bag there is a whole treasure. He contemplates what to do with it. First he attempts to put the bag on his back, but he cannot lift it because the bag is very heavy. He decides to load the contents of the bag on his wagon. First he takes out the few Khales (Jewish bread for the Sabbath) and a huge roasted duck and places them carefully on the wagon. Then he takes out a few packs of tea labelled 'W. Wissotzky' and a sizeable chunk of crystallized sugar labelled 'L. Brodtzky,' and carries them to the wagon. Next he takes dresses, expensive silk dresses, winter and summer clothing out of the bag. He also pulls out children's wear – seven outfits which coincides exactly with the number of his children. He counts the clothes admiringly and places everything on his wagon."[43]

Tevye is woken from his daydream by the hollers of two ladies who have lost their way in the woods. He takes them in his wagon and brings them to their house in the nearby resort town. At the end of the film Tevye consults Golde as to what to do with the money he received as a reward from their rich family. He starts daydreaming again, and a sequence of pictures appear on the screen which shows his dreams of fortune in a dizzy spiral.

"First Sequence - Tevye owns a new wagon and a pair of freshly shod horses.

Second Sequence - Tevye is a bread merchant. Tevye is in the bread business. He has a granary scale and granary sacks.

Third Sequence - On the river bank there is an immense pile of sacks full of bread. Tevye walks around and gives orders. All this is his. Tevye is a wholesaler.

Fourth Sequence - A huge steam-mill with a sign on it 'The Tevye Mill.' Tevye owns a mill.

Fifth Sequence - A huge elegant shop. In the entrance is a sign 'Department Store of the Merchant from the First Guild.' Tevye is a businessman, a dealer in textiles.

Sixth Sequence – A bank. A huge sign says 'Tevye and Associates Inc.' Tevye is a banker.[44]

Other aspects of Tevye's fantasy which are given visual expression in the script are demonic figures reflecting his superstitions. After Tevye has lifted the two ladies who lost their way onto the wagon, his horse stands rooted in place and refuses to move. The caption on the screen tells us the thought that crosses Tevye's mind:

"Who knows, maybe they are spirits and not women."[45]

After the caption the following sequence appears:

"He looks at his travel companions with increasing doubts. In fact, he would like to get rid of them but he doesn't know how. And indeed, at that moment the picture changes. The two women become terrible witches who approach him with their gnarled hands, and in a split second they put him on a huge broom which lifts him to the sky. Tevye doesn't despair."[46]

At this point the following caption appears on the screen:

"He knows a special incantation against satanic delusion."[47]

After the caption comes the following sequence:

"Tevye hides his face in his hands and whispers something swaying to and fro as in prayer, and indeed, the witches suddenly disappear, and two young beautiful women, with angelic faces appear instead. They move around him in a seductive dance, tickle him under his armpit, braid his beard, and try to take off his overcoat, but Tevye remains unmoved, does not surrender and does not stop his incantation. Tevye angrily says the incantation, 'Sinai and Sansinai and Samenglof – Tfu, Tfu, Tfu!' And the witches withdraw, hiding their faces in their hands. Tevye is rescued, a happy smile of victory on his face."[48]

Sholem Aleichem's fantasy takes a visual shape on the screen as does his humor. Tevye dreams that he is a banker who meets his colleague Rothschild for business. Tevye hands Rothschild his visiting card. The card has only one word on it: "TEVYE". The meeting with Rothschild has yet another comic feature. Tevye discusses business with Rothschild in the latter's luxurious office. Sholem Aleichem adds an acting direction to the script:

"Tevye holds Rothschild by the lapel of his coat."[49]

The meeting with Rothschild is described as if it takes place on a street corner of a *shtetl*, a Jewish little town. The use of the mannerism of the *shtetl* (holding one's lapel as a means of persuasion) while transacting big business creates the comic clash of the scene.

Sholem Aleichem proved that he had a great deal of visual perception in the adaptation of the script for film. The lack of a substantial final scene is therefore strongly felt. The script ends when Tevye wakes up from his daydreams and asks Golde what to do with the money. The caption on the screen says:

"What do you think Golde, do we have enough money to buy a cow, and open some business, like for instance selling milk and dairy products?"[50]

The open ending was more appropriate to the style of the serials in the Yiddish newspapers than it was for film. Newspapers used it to get their readers hooked on a sequel. Sholem Aleichem might have had the same marketing strategy in mind. Indeed he wrote another film script, *Hava - Tevye's Daughter*,[51] which related further events concerning Tevye and his household.

## Hava – Tevye's Daughter

Here too Sholem Aleichem developed the visual possibilities of the story. Sholem Aleichem raises the possibility that the parable of the poor man's lamb (The Book of Samuel) mentioned by Tevye in the play, be visualized in the film.

Sholem Aleichem makes extensive use of a film device - the flashback. Each time Tevye thinks of Hava, his reflections appear on the screen in the form of pictures from the past which show the childhood and youth of his beloved daughter.

Another change that the drama undergoes in the transition to film is probably geared to the difference in audience. The play was written for Jewish spectators, whereas the silent movie was also intended for Gentiles. This may also be the reason why Sholem Aleichem made the scoundrel that helped to rob Tevye of his daughter the village elder, not the priest. Sholem Aleichem probably did not want to show the representative of the church to the censors, the producers, and the public in a negative light. In the Yiddish speaking film of Maurice Schwartz, intended for an exclusively Jewish audience, the priest is once again the villain.

Joking in a letter to Dovid Pinsky about the sensational melodramas which characterized the repertoire of the Yiddish theater, Sholem Aleichem promised that his dramatic adaptation of Tevye would be exempt from:

"Bombastic effects, burlesque jokes, patriotic couplets, dead children, and the like."[52]

Although faithful to his artistic credo in the play, Sholem Aleichem broke his promise in his screen adaptation. The end of the script is sensational and tear-jerking. Hava can no longer bear the behavior of the peasants towards Tevye, and she throws herself into the well of her father's garden. Fedya and Tevye pull her out of the well. Golde faints and falls over her daughter's dead body. Fedya, the husband who harassed her about her Jewishness, is now crying.

Only Tevye pulls himself together and says the traditional prayer for the dead. The caption on the screen reads:
"Blessed be the true judge."[53]

The fact that in the very same year (1914) Sholem Aleichem wrote two dramatic versions of his novel *Tevye*, one a literary drama, and the other a tear-jerking film script, could perhaps testify to an adjustment of the writer to commercial considerations.

As we recall Sholem Aleichem ended his drama, *Stempenyu*, (which premiered in New York, 1907) with the suicide of its heroine. This ending which complied with the wishes of his backers in the Yiddish Theater, was in absolute contradiction to the resolution of the conflict in the novel. After years of contact with the world of show business, Sholem Aleichem probably tailored the film script to the demands of its potential buyers.

## *Tevye* – The Film by Maurice Schwartz

Maurice Schwartz directed the film version of *Tevye*[44] and played the title role. The film released in 1939, is based on Berkowitz's adaptation of Sholem Aleichem's play. The interfaith marriage of Hava, and Tevye's expulsion from the village are, as in Sholem Aleichem's play, the climax of the film.

Maurice Schwartz, the star of the Yiddish stage, turned out to be a resourceful film director. He used film language to create dramatic tension. The confrontation between Tevye and the priest is presaged in the comparison of their respective horses. Tevye's thin, shabby horse stands in stark contrast to the priest's plump, shiny beast.

In the conversation with Tevye, the priest brings up the topic of intermarriage. The priest pretends to have a conversation for the sake of conversation. Tevye plays along, but the abrupt transition from the close up of the priest to that of Tevye, and from Tevye to Golde and Hava, shows the intensity of the underlying conflict at stake. Shooting the scene from a distance, (a long shot) encompassing all the characters in one frame, would have created a misleading image of harmony.

The shattering of Hava's romantic dreams is visualized in the dinner scene with her husband's family. Except for Hava, all the members of the family, eat in a revolting manner.

Her loneliness becomes even more apparent when her husband Fedya, the only person she can talk to in this family, falls asleep on the bed with his boots on.

Maurice Schwartz wisely added comic moments to relieve from time to time the dramatic tension. The comical appearance of the clerk who accompanies the district officer, and who hands Tevye the legal documents, makes the act of expulsion look ridiculous. The clerk, the representative of the imperial bureaucracy, limps around with a bottle of ink hanging on this chest and a goose feather in his hand. This way Schwartz created an interesting tension between the tragic deed and its ludicrous perpetrators.

A few sequences of the film are theatrical. The actress who plays Tseitl puts her hands on her heart to express anxiety. The sequence of Golde's death also gets a melodramatic touch, when the face of Hava, the lost daughter, appears in the window. Her face is wet with tears and with the rain which beats down mercilessly upon her. The family inside the house does not even notice her.

The quick flashback, in which the dying Golde sees images from her life, appears to us as a worn out cliché. However these exceptions do not detract from Schwartz's unique achievement. His direction is for the most part touching and in good taste.

The sequence in Tevye's house after Hava's conversion, is free of pathos and is directed with skill. Tevye prays because, as he says: "One doesn't play angry with God". His lips move mechanically to the familiar verses as he walks aimlessly to the window. He glances for a second in the direction of the road, as if he expects an imaginary messenger who will tell him that Hava's conversion was but a bad dream. It is only when he takes the stool in order to sit *shiva* that he stumbles for a second, overcome by his emotions.

Another emotionally charged scene, that Schwartz directed expressively yet with restraint is Tevye's departure from his home. After he receives the expulsion order, Tevye stands in the empty room that had been his home for so many years. In this room, he raised his daughters. In this room his wife died. He turns his back to the camera, and his shoulders rise for a second in a silent sob after which he turns his face back to the camera. Schwartz showed the intensity of Tevye's pain without a sigh, without a single tear.

Schwartz's film version of *Tevye* is surprising even today, in its freshness and good taste. Schwartz showed that the magic of Sholem Aleichem works not only in a colorful, grotesque rendition à la Granovsky, but also as is, by letting the original text speak for itself. Schwartz's film cannot compete in the market place with *Fiddler on the Roof*, first, because of the technical gap created by the years and secondly, because the combination of fine acting with the richness of the Sholem Aleichem's dialogue, creates an excitement fully understood only to people versed in the Yiddish language and culture. Still the film is now shown successfully through various distribution avenues, such as cable television cultural centers, campuses, and film festivals.

## *Tevye* – the musical

Joseph Stein adapted the *Tevye* stories as a musical first entitled *Tevye*, then renamed *Fiddler On The Roof*, the musical premiered at the Imperial Theater in New York, on September 22, 1964. A tone of lightness prevails in the adaptation. Firstly, nothing really tragic happens in the musical version. Tseitl marries the poor tailor Motl, but, whereas in the original text Motl dies of poverty and illness, Stein's Motl lives in perfect health, and even becomes the owner of a mechanical sewing machine. Hava does indeed convert to Christianity and marries a Goy (non Jew), but the Goy is not so terrible. The proof: he decides to leave the village because he cannot go on living there after the Jews have been expelled. With such a philo-semitic husband, Hava's inter-faith marriage is hardly a disaster. Subsequently, Golde has no reason to fall sick and die.

Even the expulsion from the village is a blessing in disguise. Tevye and his wife leave the village for a better place: America. Stein's adaptation is true to the principle of mass consumption as applied to the arts. It is based on the principle of the consumer's comfort. The spectator is not asked to make any emotional or intellectual effort to reach Sholem Aleichem. Sholem Aleichem's work is processed until it becomes agreeable to the all-American taste. In this spirit, the relationship between Pertshik and Hodl is given a touch of romantic film-comedy with goodnight kisses at the door, and Hodl amorously teasing Pertshik who takes the Russian revolution a little too seriously.

Tevye too is Americanized. His daughters' romances generate in him a renewed blossoming, and with the generous back up of the orchestra, he asks Golde, "Do you love me?" A Jewish couple at the turn of the century in a small Ukrainian village would not discuss the state of their romance, but as Sholem Aleichem put it: "What can you do when America gives an order?"

Stein added sit-com routines to the text. One of many examples is Tevye's answer to the butcher, Lazar Wolf, who wants to marry his daughter:

"Lazar Wolf: Talking about the great world, how goes it with your brother-in-law in America?

Tevye: I believe he is doing very well.

Lazar: He wrote you?

Tevye: Not lately.

Lazar: Then how do you know?

Tevye: Because he has not written!...If he needed help, we would surely hear."[46]

Stein's adaptation also has good qualities. Stein is a professional. His stage instincts are sharp. His timing, excellent. The lines are concentrated and always move the plot forward. Stein is a librettist for whom the text is only one ingredient. It must blend with the music and the image. The craftsman, Stein, fared better than the artist Sholem Aleichem in his stage writing technique. Sholem Aleichem looked for actors and directors that could serve his text. Stein took a symmetrically opposed attitude. He looked in the Sholem Aleichem text for elements that can serve the theater.

Stein's dialogues flow. The other ingredients of the musical blend and fill the intentional gaps of the text. The actor can talk less and act more. Stein let the music and dance seduce the eyes and ears of his audience.

To his credit, Stein is entertaining. In one of the scenes he added, Pertshik taught the Bible to Tevye's daughters in a Marxist interpretation. The lines are not without charm.

"Beylke: But why did Laban fool Jacob and give him his ugly daughter, Lea?

Pertshik: (to Shprintse) Do you know why?

Shprintse: Because she was oldest.

Pertshik: No, because he wanted more work from him. Because that is the way of an employer, remember that children, you can never trust an employer.

Beylke: That's what the Bible teaches us?

Pertshik: That's what the Bible teaches us."[47]

## *Fiddler On The Roof* – The Film

The film released in 1971, was also written by Joseph Stein.[48] It is almost a copy of the musical, and has the same qualities and shortcomings. Naturally, the medium engenders a more extensive use of audio visual elements. Thus the setting can be extended beyond the four walls of the theater. The opening scene of the film does just that: The camera pans over a range of fields creating the feeling of a never ending Ukrainian landscape. The sound of a violin creeps into the image as the camera discovers a fiddler on a roof. The fiddler, a symbol of the precarious Jewish existence in Eastern Europe, becomes the leitmotif of the film.

The film allowed Tevye's monologues to be visualized. The script took full advantage of the possibilities offered by the camera. In the middle of the dialogue with Lazar Wolf, the butcher, the frame freezes on the butcher's face. Time stops, and Tevye (Haim Topol), has the opportunity to reassess the situation. He deliberates whether he should give his daughter to the butcher by means of a simulated dialogue with the camera, that is, with the audience. When this is done, the camera returns to the butcher, and the film goes on.

Tevye's fantasies become visual treats as in the sequence in which Tevye tells his wife about the appearance of the butcher's late wife in his dream. More than half a century since Sholem Aleichem wrote the film script *Hava - Tevye's Daughter* yet another of his artistic visions was fulfilled. As we recall, a substantial part of the script visualized Tevye's dreams and fantasies.

In spite of all its shortcomings the film kept the essence of Sholem Aleichem's play: the breaking up of a family in a changing world. Stein, like Sholem Aleichem before him, understood that only the story of a specific family will create a general interest. It is by making a very Jewish film that he made a film of universal appeal.

## *Tevye* and the critics – The play by Maurice Schwartz

Mr. Vladek, the theater critic of the Forward opened his article by describing the public's embarrassment during the premiere, in which it had to deal with a serious play by Sholem Aleichem. According to the critic the public expected only comedy from Sholem Aleichem.

"Throughout the performance on Friday night, watching the play, and also while leaving the theater, the public could not make up its mind as to whether the play was a success or not, and of how they should relate to it. The main reason for this uncertainty was the fact that they did not expect a serious drama from Sholem Aleichem. Everybody knows Sholem Aleichem as the great Jewish humorist."[49]

The critic developed his claim in a somewhat bizarre way. Since Tevye is known as "one of Sholem Aleichem's most successful comic types"[50], the serious tone of the play was even more surprising. Somebody who had not read Sholem Aleichem's *Tevye* might get the impression from Vladek's article that the comical Tevye of the stories became a tragic figure in the drama. The truth of the matter is that Tevye had a sense of humor but was never comical neither in the original stories, nor in the drama. Sholem Aleichem did not change the essence of the character in the transition from literature to drama.

On second thought, the critic of the Forward found his surprise a pleasant one. He discovered that Sholem Aleichem was also dramatically gifted.

Vladek noticed that the Jewish theater of the time was flooded with plays that dealt with the Jewish problem. *Tevye*, in his opinion, was the best among them.

As for the performance, the critic praised the acting of Maurice Schwartz as Tevye. In contrast, he found the acting of Berta Gersten, in the role of Hava, weak. The critic felt that Hava's inner struggle was not visible in Berta Gersten's acting. The same applied to the actor Tannenholz in the role of Fedya. The two, Gersten and Tannenholz, gave the impression that they did not know the text and waited for help from the prompter. The critic ended his article with praise for the stage scenery. He was especially impressed by the first act in which live pigeons and chickens helped creating a genuine village atmosphere.

## The Critics and The Film by Maurice Schwartz

Mr. Fogelman, who wrote the review for the Forward thought that adapting *Tevye* for the screen was a bad idea. In his words:

"A work that is written in the genre of a novel has its own rules which are completely different from the rules of a play or those of a film. Once you cut a play or a film from such a work the operation must take a lot of blood and strength from the original work."[51]

He went on in his preface to the article:

"Also, in my opinion, it is very difficult, if not impossible, to create an authentic play with suspense and dramatic action from Sholem Aleichem's touching, lyrical, and humorous novel, *Tevye*."[52]

Those opening lines are somewhat puzzling. From what Fogelman wrote, one could assume that Schwartz adapted *Tevye* for the first time. Actually, Sholem Aleichem himself adapted *Tevye* as a play, on which the film was based.

Throughout the long article, Schwartz is not blamed for the weakness of the film. The Sholem Aleichem material, as previously mentioned, did not lend itself to dramatization.

In an unexpected reversal, the critic's final conclusion is a positive one. Primarily, because Fogelman felt that in the film, Maurice Schwartz reached the highest level of acting.

"I can't imagine a better Tevye than the one portrayed for us by Schwartz."[53]

He also found the mass scenes to be good. The film, Mr. Fogelman summed up was:

"one of the best Yiddish films ever made."[54]

## The critics and Tevye in Habima – 1944 and 1950

The critic, Luvrani, opened his article emphasizing the relevance of *Tevye* as a symbol of the Jewish people's struggle for survival. The play was staged in 1944, a time of the greatest distress ever known to the Jewish nation.

"Though Tevye is presented to us in bad times, it is the right time for it. In normal times we might have been a little impatient with him and his incessant shower of commentaries. But since the Germans assault him and want to turn him to ashes, our hearts open to him with pity and love."[55]

Luvrani complained about Berkowitz's adaptation which deprived the play of the lyrical touch of the original. He regretted the extreme polarization between Jews and Gentiles in the adaptation.

"But I'm not sure whether Berkowitz did the right thing in presenting Tevye as tense from the very start. He prevents us from understanding how much Tevye is part of this landscape, and in what great pain he is when he has to leave it. We did not see the Tevye who enjoys trees and fields, the Tevye, who in fact, lives a good life with the Gentiles. Here he stands in front of us, with the immigration papers for Palestine searing his soul."[56]

The critic also felt that Berkowitz's adaptation lacked not only good taste but that it also hurt the credibility of the characters and adulterated the dramatic action.

"Furthermore, one wonders how this world could appeal to a delicate soul like Hava, Tevye's daughter. The Gentiles presented to us are partly stupid, partly evil, and mostly both stupid and evil."[57]

However, the critic also found a positive side to the production in the director's work. Although not perfect, it did show an intimate knowledge of the subject:

"Chemerinsky is at home in this landscape. He knows how to make it accessible and real. In his hands, this corner of Jewish existence in the Diaspora was made full of life and charm."[58]

The same phenomenon that characterized the best performances of Tevye in the Yiddish theater, appeared in the revival of *Tevye* at the Israeli National Theater, Habima in 1950. It seems that *Tevye* was not a dramatic piece that needed sophisticated directing or exquisite stage design. The Habima actor, Bertonov, like Maurice Schwartz before him, performed the main role masterfully and carried the entire performance on his shoulders. The critic in <u>Devar Hapoelet</u>, opened his review with an apology to the other actors because he must ignore them.

"The other members of Habima who played their roles in the festive performance of *Tevye* should forgive me, but on this evening, the audience saw only one actor, the seventy-year-old Yehoshua Bertonov. And it seemed that the rest of the players, came up on the stage mainly to help the hero of the evening, and that they too concentrated on the sublime acting of their colleague. Sholem Aleichem's play is without inventions, without technical surprises, without intellectual tension, and without complicated analysis. Just the life of a Jew and a man. The life of Tevye. Sholem Aleichem, the writer of the Diaspora, loved the strange life of his people, like other writers loved the life of their nations. And thanks to the simple acting, free of eloquence and declamation, the wonderful everyday acting of Bertonov, came the satisfaction of a soul full to the rim, that only nature and genuine art can give. There was a perfection in his acting that inspired you to believe him." [59]

Bertonov, like Schwartz, played the role in an understated, restrained manner, and thereby elicited deep emotional reaction from the spectators.

"Although the scenes that displayed pathos conquered the audience, it was really the fine allusions of an expression, of a movement, of a look, modest allusions, almost hidden, that touched the Jewish soul."[60]

*Tevye* is apparently a play that carries a tremendous emotional load which comes from both the Sholem Aleichem text, and the historical context in which it is presented. In both America and Russia of the war years, Tevye's struggle had an existential significance for the audience. The production in Habima in 1950, in the newly founded Jewish state, gave, at least to the critic, a feeling of a profound significance transcending the play and the theater. Tevye became a symbol of the many hardships experienced by the Jews until they realized their spiritual and political independence.

"Everybody present at this event was, so it seemed, thinking to himself: From the loneliness, alienation, the abandonment of Tevye in his native village, what abysses were crossed until this point was reached."[61]

The performance, from this point of view, appeared to be a an artistic as well as a national catharsis.

"Because the abandonment of the Jews is over, there is support for the people and there is a people for the Jewish artist...In this evening, the glory of art and the glory of national independence blended and impassioned the spectators."[62]

## The Moscow Critics

The Soviet critics dedicated enthusiastic articles to the performance of *Tevye* in the Moscow Jewish State Theater. Upon reading the review written by Peretz Markish in his book about Mikhoels, one is made aware of the embarrassing excesses in Soviet journalistic and literary criticism. The tone is that of superlative praise combined with crude use of criticism for purposes of political propaganda.

If one is to believe the Soviet critics, then the essence of Tevye's personality was in fact a yearning for the establishment of a Soviet regime in Russia. Markish wrote:

"In Tevye, Mikhoels objectively demonstrates the childhood of the century. Now Mikhoels has once again to climb a mountain. He has to reach the middle and ripe years of our century, and the making of the new Socialist Jew, not in Tevye anymore, but in Tevye's sons, in the newborn sons of the great Jewish people, who together with the best sons of all nations fulfilled and realized the dream of the Tevyes, of the oppressed masses. And we have full hope, that the artistic height that Mikhoels reached in Tevye, is once more a threshold to new and greater artistic heights. This is how Mikhoels presented the concept of Tevye."[63]

## *Tevye* – Epilogue

The Jewish theater was unique in that the history of one play mirrored the political and artistic turmoil of the century. The various interpretations of the play take us from the realistic lyrical interpretation of Maurice Schwartz in the Yiddish theater in New York, to the restrictive imperatives of the Soviet theater under Stalin, through the nationalistic approach of Berkowitz, and finally to the jazzed up Broadway production.

Unlike the Sholem Aleichem comedies, which use visual comic effects, a wide collection of characters, movement and music, *Tevye*, the drama, relies almost exclusively on the Sholem Aleichem text and the actors who perform it.

In this type of production, the theater shrinks to a triangle composed of text, director, and actor. Occasionally, one discovers that a forbidden relationship has developed between the actor and the text, behind the director's back. The director's instructions were different in different times and places, but various performers bypassed them when necessary. An identical sensitivity led them intuitively to the spirit of the original Sholem Aleichem text.

# 6. The Jackpot

*The Jackpot* [*Dos Groyse Gevins*] was written by an ailing Sholem Aleichem in 1915, a year before his death. It is Sholem Aleichem's best comedy. Maybe because, by that time, he had gained experience in dramatic writing. However, contrary to the common myth that Sholem Aleichem wrote effortlessly, *The Jackpot* was not written in one draft. The manuscript[1] is covered with layers of changes written on paper strips, neatly cut and glued. Sholem Aleichem did not leave, and probably did not write more than one version of the play. He did write however additional versions for acts three and four. The difference between them and the final version of the play can be found in the portrayal of the tailor's daughter, Beylke.

### The Difference in Beylke

In the two rejected versions the tailor's daughter Beylke is completely passive. The two apprentices who are in love with her, do everything for her and she just follows. This is in contrast with the character of young women in Sholem Aleichem plays. The young women in Sholem Aleichem's dramas are educated and have independent personalities as exemplified by Hava in *Tevye*. In *The Treasure* Esther does not openly rebel against her father, but she ends up marrying the man of her, not his choice.

*Tevye* takes place in a village. *The Treasure* takes place in a little town. *The Jackpot* is an urban comedy. (In *The Treasure* we have a money-lender, whereas in *The Jackpot* we have a bank). Sholem

Aleichem himself specified the setting of *The Jackpot* as "A Jewish town in the old country",[2] contrary to the "little town" [3] "shtetl"as the location of *The Treasure*.

It seems that on second thought Sholem Aleichem decided to change the passive character of Beylke. It was hardly plausible that she, the city girl, would be less self reliant than her sisters in the little town and village.

## The Hebrew Version of I.D. Berkowitz

Just as in his adaptations of *Tevye* and *The Treasure* Berkowitz came up with a more dynamic version of *The Jackpot*[5] but here too, the change was not limited to the form. Berkowitz also changed the content of the play.

Let us begin with the structural changes. In the original play the tailor Saroker loses the jackpot's money to two crooks who offer him a partnership in a phoney movie business. The story of the fraud opens as a play within a play, and Berkowitz cut it out completely. The plot became more homogenous, but the character of Shimele lost psychological depth. In Berkowitz's version Shimele loses his money over a technicality. The bank simply made a mistake. This turn of events is arbitrary, and does not tell us anything about Shimele's personality. The fact that he loses his money in an industry that sells illusions is not without significance. Shimele is a man of dreams. He wins his money in one factory of dreams, the lottery, and loses it in another factory of dreams, the movies. Shimele like Levy Mozgovyer and Stempenyu is a visionary. In Berkowitz's version this point is blurred.

## Berkowitz Introduces Starker Contrasts

Berkowitz thought that Sholem Aleichem's text needed sharper contrasts and tougher action. Koltun the manager of the apartment shows interest in Beylke in the Sholem Aleichem version. In the Berkowitz version he puts his hands on her:

"Motl: You fool, I'm serious...(looks through the window) Here comes Beylke. (stands up and looks) Look at this, he is harassing her once more, the bastard!
Kopl (stands up): Who?
Motl: Don't you know who? The manager.
Kopl: (runs to the window) Koltun?
Motl: Look how he blocks her way, pulls her by the hand...What a low life! What a monster!"[5]

In Berkowitz's version Koltun becomes so rude that even Shimele jumps on him, infuriated.

"Shimele: (in rage) Listen to me. As long as you tyrannize me and my wife, I can take it. That is I'll get back at you, with God's will, later... But don't you put your hands on my daughter! Do you hear what I am saying to you? She is my one and only daughter!"[6]

The conflict between the contenders for Beylke's hand in Berkowitz's version, also became sharper. Berkowitz vilifies and degenerates the character of Solomon Fein, the rich man's son. Solomon who is described as a "handsome young man"[7] in Sholem Aleichem's play, becomes in Berkowitz's version "An ugly old bachelor"[8] with a rheumatic illness in his right hand. Berkowitz exhibits Solomon's handicap in a scene in which he tries on a suit in the tailors workshop.

The exchange of words between Beylke and Solomon Fein becomes more acrimonious as well. In the original play Beylke does not want to marry him simply because she is in love with the apprentice tailor. In Berkowitz's version she also resents the trouble he gave her in the past:

"Solomon: (after a pause) Is that so, ha ha...May I ask, mademoiselle Sarokin, whether you find your stay in the new apartment a pleasant one?
Beylke: In the new apartment? I don't know...(suddenly looks at him) Did they pay you the rent yet?"[9]

The Sarokers too, once they become rich, are mercilessly ridiculed by Berkowitz. The nouveau riche Shimele Saroker puts a fancy new book cabinet with no books in his living room.

Sholem Aleichem ridiculed his wife:

"On her neck pearls, big diamond earrings on her ears, all eight fingers sparkle with rings."[10]

Berkowitz made her look even more ridiculous:

"Eti Meni shows up, adorned with necklaces and golden earrings. Her wig is awry and her face shines and glows."[11]

In Berkowitz's adaptation even the physical action is rough. When Motl and Kopl visit the new house of Shimele, Koltun approaches Motl and brutally takes the hat off his head, so that he may speak with a bare head to Shimele, the new rich man in town.

Berkowitz was not a man of nuances or half tones. The angry characters became angrier and the sweet characters became sweeter.

In an effort to reshape the characters Berkowitz changed their environment. With Sholem Aleichem the story takes place in a realistic urban surrounding ("a Jewish town in the old country").[12] Berkowitz preferred the enchanted literary fiction of Kasrilevke.[13] In the transition from the town to the *shtetl*, Beylke becomes a helpless provincial girl.

In Sholem Aleichem's play it is Beylke who comes up with the idea of eloping to prevent her marriage to Solomon Fein. In Berkowitz's version it is Motl's idea, and Beylke accepts it as a last resort. Furthermore, in Berkowitz's version they plan to elope to Beylke's cousin's home, which makes the elopement look less scandalous. The wedding of Motl and Beylke is delayed in Berkowitz's version until Shimele Saroker finds his daughter and gives his consent to the marriage. In short, Berkowitz's Beylke is a lot closer to the ideal of a nice Jewish daughter. The changes that Berkowitz introduced reflect his middle class moral concepts.

Berkowitz's non realistic approach is apparent also in the time-set of the play. He omitted Sholem Aleichem's concrete time ("before the war"),[14] and left the play hanging in the timelessness of a fairy tale.

In Berkowitz's version the play becomes a fairy tale for adults. When the characters are good, they are very good, but when they are bad, they are horrid.

## *The Jackpot* in Moscow

Alexander Granovsky directed "200,000" [*The Jackpot*] at the Moscow Jewish State Theater in 1923. He changed the face of the Russian Jewish theater, which until that time presented mainly shund plays and worked in compliance with the star system. In shund theater, the text is of no consequence, and the only thing that counts is the star. The theater is a medium that enables the star to carry on a private affair with the audience. In shund performances, to this day, the public applauds their favorite actors whenever they appear on stage in complete disregard of the play or the other actors on stage. The idea of stage discipline was and is alien to the Yiddish shund theater - every actor tries to outplay the others and hopefully steal the show. Granovsky brought to the Jewish theater the idea of stage discipline and team work. Innovative theatrical concepts characterized his work. Sholem Aleichem's drama found in him an unorthodox but inspiring interpreter.

### Granovsky Changes the Characters

John Galsworthy remarked that character is dramatic situation. This is true of Sholem Aleichem's drama. If Shimele Saroker was not a dreamer he would not have lost his money in a dubious venture. He would not have won the money in the first place either. All those events which make up the totality of the play happen to Shimele because he is the kind of man he is. Koltun, the manager of Fein's houses, is a reasonable person who knows that lottery tickets do not win. He would never have gambled on a lottery ticket and won. In Sholem Aleichem's plays not only characters determine events, but events never change characters. Othello is not the same Othello he was before the discovery of the handkerchief. Tevye, on the other hand, is always the same Tevye. He stands like a rock in a sea of change. Hence the key to any interpretation of Sholem Aleichem's plays is on the first page, in the list of characters. The differences in the directorial concepts lie in different perceptions of the characters.

Granovsky started with a new division of the characters. Sholem Aleichem did not ignore the class differences in Jewish society, but what really mattered to him was the individual, not his social class. The visionary tailor, his petty wife, the stingy rich man Fein, they all attracted Sholem Aleichem equally. Granovsky sifted all the characters through a filter of class. The Soviet critic Litvakov explained:

"For the first time a Jewish social comedy of significant proportion was created. Sholem Aleichem's comedy of manners cannot fill the grandiose proportion of Granovsky. Sholem Aleichem's lyrical humor and dreamy skepticism remained contained only in the petit bourgeois nucleus of the play, in the characters of Shimele Saroker, Soloveitchik the matchmaker and others, that is in the very environment that Sholem Aleichem knew and felt for so thoroughly. For the two external flanks, for the working people on one side, and for the money people on the other, the theater found a completely different rhythm, taken this time not from Sholem Aleichem, but from the way of life and ideology of the October Revolution."[15]

Granovsky assimilated the specificity of the individual character into the generality of the social class. Under his direction Kopl and Motl were, first and foremost, representatives of the proletarian class. They were no longer just two young men in love with one woman, the one perplexed and slow, the other energetic and outspoken.

### *Tableaux Vivants*

Granovsky shifted the emphasis of the Sholem Aleichem play from the individual character to his social group. Each Sholem Aleichem character has a linguistic style of his own. In order to merge the characters into a larger picture of a social group Granovsky had to play down the text and introduce other, non verbal elements to the stage. Dobrushin in his book about the actor Binyomin Zuskin describes the devices Granovsky used, in order to free himself from Sholem Aleichem's overpowering text. One device is a sequence of *tableaux vivants* where the actors are used as visual elements of a picture rather than as mouthpieces for the text. Another non-verbal device is the use of body language, in addition to the written text. In Dobrushin words:

"In its first works on the classical Yiddish repertoire the Moscow Jewish State Theater looked for directorial devices, that helped it rely less on the dramatic word and dialogue and more on the explicit colorful *mise en scène*. The theater gave more attention to the live pictures which were constantly rearranged with large groups of actors, and even to the movement of the bodies in space and to the plastic expression of the individual actors."[16]

Litvakov described in his book, *Five Years Jewish State Chamber Theater* [*Finf Yor Melukhisher Yidisher Kamer Teater*] how Granovsky squeezed the rich men into one collective picture of the Jewish Bourgeoisie. The different characters are shown in a single negative light.

"The rich men face each other in two rows, (old and new rich) touch hands, thus forming an arch under which pass a line of marionette like rich men with bent backs. A street cleaner's broom swings over all of them - as a satiric symbol of both their ascendancy and their pending doom."[17]

The scene exemplifies the use of the live pictures, where props and actors are thrown together into one visual composition. The animate and inanimate blend into one morbid picture of a dying class:

"And when by a dim light the half dead figures of the chaotic world of the rich go to the table accompanied by a somber tune, played apathetically by Chagallesque musicians, one gets the impression of a funeral dance in the burial procession of a dead social class."[18]

Litvakov added with Jacobean ardor:

"This goes far beyond the strict framework of a Jewish comedy, this is already a universal comedy, where the bourgeoisie is actually being guillotined by the social satire of the October era."[19]

## Class Division – Space Division

Granovsky divided the characters of the play into two opposing categories as did another ideological theater: The medieval one.[20] The characters in Granovsky's interpretation are divided into good and bad. In the Medieval theater the spiritual division is expressed by a physical division of the stage into two levels. The upper level is paradise and the lower level is hell. On the upper level God sits surrounded by white winged angels singing hallelujah in celestial harmony, and on the low level Satan and his devils dwell amid the smoke of boiling tar and the screams of the penitent sinners.

Granovsky divided the stage in a similar manner. In his theater the proletarians took the place of the angels, and the bourgeoisie that of Satan. The working class sat on the top of the stage, and the capitalists at the bottom.

Granovsky used constructivist stage design for that purpose. Conventional stage design serves as a background and is intended to give an illusion of a location such as a forest or a street. In Granovsky's production the stage design was a construction that the actors could sit on, jump from, and hang onto.

In pictures from the production[21] we can see that the rich men are always down, in the low, earthy level of the stage. Their full bellies and fat buttocks pull them downward. In contrast, the workers jump joyfully on the high planks of the set. In the workshop scenes the stage space is open, and one has the sensation of freedom.

In the salon scenes the space is enclosed with planks and drapes thereby creating a feeling of suffocation.

The movement of the actors is in harmony with the stage design. The rich men move with their limbs drooping down. The movement of the laborers flow in symmetrical opposition, always upwards. In the tailor's shops the workers have straight backs, their arms vigorously lifted up in choreographed movements as they sew with imaginary needles and threads. This way Granovsky created an identification of work with joy.

## Beyond the Text

Granovsky did not use the actors as interpreters of the text, but as commentators that gave it new meaning. Granovsky gave the actors:
"The ability to add layers of meanings to the words through illustrative acting devices, and thereby to change the meaning of the lines. The new meanings that the theater had endeavored to bring out of the text of the classics characterized the method and style of the theater."[22]

One of Granovsky's acting devices became almost a trade mark of Jewish theater and film: The flying matchmaker. Soloveitchik the matchmaker is a *luftmentsh*, that is someone who wheels and deals with nothing, with thin air. Soloveytchik appeared in Granovsky's production, hanging in the air, swinging between heaven and earth, jumping with his umbrella on the town's roofs.

Granovsky managed to free himself from the dictatorship of Sholem Aleichem's text by creating a physical stage language parallel to the Sholem Aleichem lines. This calls to mind Artaud's experiments.[23] Artaud regarded the text as a literary, non-theatrical element. In his attempt to shake the hitherto uncontested predominance of the written word on stage, Artaud offered to use a language of theatrical symbols, much like notes in music. These theatrical signs would replace the verbal text. As an example of this new kind of theater Artaud used the non verbal language of the Balinese theater. In the Balinese theater evening is presented in the following manner: The actor imitates a bird who sits on a tree with one eye open and the other already closed. Artaud suggested ideographs as the name for the visual signs that would make up the new theatrical language. If the Western theater succeeded to free itself from the subjugation to the written word, it could in time make up a whole inventory of autonomous stage symbols that, similarly to the ancient Egyptian hieroglyphs, would form a complete language. The theater would then have what literature, music, and the plastic arts, have achieved: A language of its own.

In the imaginary encounter between Artaud and Granovsky one can find an obvious common denominator, which is the basic urge to free the theater from its dependency on the classics and their texts. The two differed however in their Techniques.

Artaud aspired to liberate the theater from the dictatorship of the word by the invention of nonverbal, visual signs, Granovsky, influenced by Chagall, turned to the words, in order to make new, non-verbal use of them.

Granovsky overlooked the usual semantics of the words and turned to their concrete, literal meaning. Soloveytchik the matchmaker has a finger in every pie. The Yiddish idiom says that he "dances at all the weddings". Granovsky therefore ordered the actor Zuskin to walk on stage in dance steps.

"The dazzling finger play of Soloveitchik is meant to demonstrate visually the illusive figure of the matchmaker. The actor Zuskin shows in a grotesque way the social character of this *luftmensh*, the nature of this eternally unsuccessful wheeler dealer. When Soloveitchik performs his dancing steps he also demonstrates the urgent need of the matchmaker to be in everyone's presence all the time, dancing, as we say, at all weddings. His movements are articulate, they even contain a subtext, they trigger associations and replace words where the director cut the text in order to give free reign to the visual and the graphic elements on stage."[24]

## Shimele Saroker – Two Ideographs

The Soviet actor and director Lubomirski describes the scene where Shimele gets the news that he has won the jackpot. Granovsky used movement as commentary on the text. The result was a powerful grotesque image.

"The scene where Saroker gets the news of the jackpot is unforgettable. Shimele is so dazzled, that his legs cave in. He is neither standing nor sitting. His daughter, Beylke, puts something on his head that looks like a sack tied at one end. Actually it is not a sack, rather a triangular *homentash* [Purim pastry]...Suddenly Saroker tears himself from his strange paralysis, straightens up, and assumes the pose of a sort of Napoleon. No more silence. He starts talking.

'You wait!' he proudly announces. 'I will show you who Shimele Saroker is, and what Shimele can do!' At first this comic metamorphosis looks wildly strange. But try to watch the Shimele character closely and the philosophy of the *nouveau riche* will unfold in front of you in all its glory."[26]

Another episode where the character of Shimele Saroker takes on a grotesque dimension through the actor's movement, takes place when Shimele signs the check that will rob him of the money he has won.

"Whoever saw the performance, will not forget the moment, when Shimele signs the check. Mikhoels demonstrates clearly what an illiterate Shimele is - even signing the check is a hard task for him. He has to make such a huge effort, that his tongue comes out of his mouth! Furthermore, in this effort he lifts his left foot off the ground. Those movements bear witness that Saroker is a big child."[27]

Granovsky took advantage of the uniqueness of the theater as a point of encounter between the concrete and the abstract, between the live actor on one hand and the written word on the other. Granovsky disturbed the *modus vivendi* between the two. He surprised his audience by making a concrete use of the abstract and an abstract use of the concrete. Under Granovsky's direction the words received a plastic dimension and the physical movement of the actor took on dramatic significance.

## Granovsky in the Service of the Revolution

Aside from the element of surprise and pleasure for the spectator, qualities important in themselves, the use of a concrete stage language was for Granovsky, the ideologically engaged director, an important asset.

The concrete elements, such as the color of the actor's hair, or the type of chair he sits on, strike our perception long before his text reaches us. The advantage of the image over the word is obvious. The very speed at which the image penetrates our consciousness enables it to escape any criticism that eventually sneaks into the process of understanding the words. This represents an important advantage for a director who wants to sell an ideology. It enables him to market his political message in an instant, before the spectator has the opportunity to make up his mind about it. This is also the reason why the Soviet, and later the Nazi directors used a concrete image language in theater and film, in a largely successful effort to engage their art in the service of their ideology.

In Granovsky's interpretation, the rich man Fine moves heavily, his huge belly thrusts forward and his short arms hardly able to move. Similarly, in Eisenstein's *Strike*,[28] the huge belly of the capitalist fills the entire armchair, and his short hand with a cigar stuck between his fingers, can hardly reach the drinks on the table in front of him. In another Eisenstein film *General Line*[29] the *kulaks*, the rich farmers, refuse to lend their plough horse to their poor neighbors. On the screen we see the two fat faces of the rich *kulak* couple, with only a double chin separating the faces from their corpulent bodies.

Capitalists are not necessarily fat but Granovsky like Eisenstein did not take time for nuances. The spectator has to grasp in a glance who's belly is full and who's is empty.

Revolutionary theater is not about words. It is about clear cut images. The ideological label had to be as poignant as the trademark on a bottle of Coca Cola.

## The Italian Comedy's Influence on Granovsky

In his search for strong theatrical modes of expression Granovsky turned to territories new to the Yiddish theater. He used sources as diverse as the comedia dell'arte[30] and Chaplin's film comedy. Granovsky absorbed the adventurous innovative spirit of the revolutionary Soviet theater, at a time when people such as Tairov Meyerhold and Eisenstein worked on the Russian theatrical scene.

The comedia dell'arte had a special influence on Granovsky's work. The Italian comedy gives an unequivocal impression of the characters by means of exaggerated dress, make up, and acting. The cast of characters is made up of stereotypes: A miser, a fornicator, a bragging captain and so forth. Granovsky used the techniques of the

Italian comedy to show his audience a social set of stereotypes: The honest worker, the mean capitalist, the unproductive matchmaker.

Granovsky was enchanted by the use of masks in the Italian comedy. The mask gives the character an immediate expression, and spare the director and the actor the construction of character by means of painstaking psychological build up. This enabled Granovsky to free himself from what he considered to be the inessential, that is the psychology of the individual character, and concentrate on the essential, namely the character's social class.

The actors under Granovsky's direction did not attempt to become one with the character, as taught by Stanislavsky, but rather present a mask, only this time a social one: That of the poor tailor or the rich landlord. The use of social masks made it easier for the spectator not to identify with the character.

The actors of the Moscow State Theater under Granovsky did not attempt to experience the feelings of the characters they portrayed. They did not embody them, they only presented them. They adopted and passed on to the spectator a detached point of view which made social criticism of the characters possible.

The parallel between the Moscow Jewish State Theater and the comedia dell'arte reveals a great deal about Granovsky's work. Like the Italians, Granovsky freed his actors from the dictatorship of the written word. The character was not only the text put in his mouth but rather the *gestus*: The movement and the mimicry. But, whereas the Italian comedians enjoyed the freedom of plays without precise texts, and could improvise as they liked, the actors of the Moscow Jewish State Theater gained little from the new disregard for the text, because in lieu of the *Diktat* of the playwright, came the *Diktat* of the director. The tyranny of the text in the bourgeois theater was replaced by the tyranny of the Soviet ideology.

## Sholem Aleichem and the Revolution

The very choice of a classical repertoire (Golfaden, Sholem Aleichem) confronted the Jewish theater with an ideological problem:

What is the relevancy of the pre-revolutionary bourgeois repertoire to the new reality of the Soviet society?

Comrade Khashin wrote with a note of concern:

"The classical repertoire presented typical characters and situations, from the past, from a finished class system, gone forever."[31]

The strict ideological principles of the Soviet Jewish Theater created a paradox: Plays by second and third rate playwrights, who wrote after the revolution, and needless to say by the rules of the revolution, obtained ideological legitimization, and were presented untouched, whereas the works of the bourgeois classics, such as Peretz and Sholem Aleichem, were routinely tampered with. In another twist of irony this turned to be a blessing in disguise. The ideologically-Kosher plays were presented in a socialist-realist manner, which was almost a sure recipe for theatrical boredom. The reactionary plays had to be worked on and subsequently became theatrical treats.

Granovsky had to prevent an identification of the public with Sholem Aleichem's bourgeois drama. The solution was found in the grotesque.

The grotesque is incongruous: Half human half demonic. This is how Granovsky wanted to present the rich. He did not want to present them as full fledged devils, because it would make them look too powerful. The public must hate the rich, not be scared of them. The grotesque offered a perfect solution: It is devilish and human, scary and laughable at the same time. The rich landlord with his thrusting belly and stove pipe hat is the incarnation of evil made ridiculous, hence laughable. True he has power and money, but his fat belly, his short arms and his huge hat remind us of a circus clown. In Khashin's words:

"Yesterday's characters were not presented from a historical perspective but from a contemporary angle. This prevented the theater from falling into the pattern of petty bourgeois realism of the Yiddish classics. The very ideological function of the theater was to tear down this pattern. Had it followed the old realistic framework, the Jewish State Theater would have remained similar to one of the

Jewish pre-revolutionary theaters, and would have been but a more accomplished version of the The Vilna Troupe or the theater of Maurice Schwartz.

The classical repertoire combined with the new Soviet approach to it, dictated the use of grotesque methods. The sharp contemporary grotesque light that the theater threw on yesterday's figures in the play, built an illusionary bridge between the reality of past literature with the Soviet present. The Moscow Yiddish State Theater did not yet have a new vocabulary for the Soviet present, but had contemporary Soviet laughter for the past."[32]

What Khashin called "The system of the grotesque" made the role of the director in the theater a central one. The written text became but a springboard for the director's fantasy. The director's prompt book turned into an autonomous entity with an affinity, but no commitment to the original text.

"The grotesque method and the strategy of social masks brought to the theater a dictatorship of theatrical fantasy. The result was a purely theatrical construction of the theme, composition, and plot of the performance. The director had his own stage composition, and his own dramatic plot, and they had little to do with the scenic composition and dramatic plot of the original play."[33]

### Granovsky Changes the Text

Granovsky reduced the Sholem Aleichem text significantly so that he could send his own theatrical message. He was a visual director and had complete mastery of the non verbal ingredients of the theater. His approach to the text was unconventional. It would, however, be a mistake to assume that Granovsky dismissed the verbal element. He valued the text. He even added text when he felt it was necessary. With the help of the adaptors Dobrushin and Oyslender, Granovsky gave Shimele, the new millionaire-tailor, a song about his new name. By means of the song Granovsky developed a motif that was already contained in the original Sholem Aleichem text: the social snobbery of the *nouveau riche*. Shimele, the new millionaire, tries to rid himself of his folksy Jewish name, and adopt a high class Russian sounding name.

"Not Shimele, not Shimele
Is now my name
My name is, my name is,
It will soon come back to me.
Semion Makarovitsh! Semion Makarovitsh!
My new name is Semion Makar,
I should be so healthy
I lost my old name
Since I became wealthy"[34]

Listening to the soundtrack of the song from the performance,[30] one discovers that Granovsky had an innovative approach to the lyrics. Words and music clash rather than agree with each other. The intended idiocy of the lyrics are made more conspicuous by the majestic musical accompaniment. Modern, Brecht like sounds, emanate from Granovsky's work.

The song in which Motl and Beylke confess their mutual love is also built on a series of contrasts.

"Beylke: By my life I swear
Motl: And I by my iron and scissors."[35]

Of all things, Motl chooses a pair of scissors upon which to swear his love. Beylke does swear by her life, but the romantic text is not accompanied by an orchestra of soft playing violins, but rather by the raw sound of a hurdy-gurdy.

Granovsky, did not want to lull the audience into a pleasant daze. He preferred to disconcert even in the traditionally mellow, romantic scenes.

Granovsky gave his own interpretation to the Sholem Aleichem text. When the text stood in opposition to his interpretation, Granovsky changed it. Dobrushin and Oyslender did the rewriting for him.

Sholem Aleichem's Shimele Saroker remains a sympathetic man despite his metamorphosis as a *nouveau riche*. His pocket and his heart are open for the needy. From Granovsky's point of view wealth equals evil. The rich Shimele is therefore evil. Since the original text says nothing of the sort, Granovsky had to add additional lines which shed negative light on Shimele Saroker.

"When the news came out that Shimele won the big win, the entire 200,000 rubles, the choir (the mob) called to each other: People say that Shimele has become a rich man.

Suddenly Motl shouts out his line: Shimele Saroker got rich - and we got a new pig in town. What a shame."[36]

## Folklore

Litvakov praised Granovsky for his lack of literary fetishism. By literary fetishism Litvakov meant the respect for literary property. Literary property is like any other property. In a socialist regime it belongs to the masses. Consequently one can do with it as one pleases.

Indeed for Granovsky, there was no difference between a Sholem Aleichem play or a folk song: Both texts served as raw material for his theatrical spectacle.

Granovsky opened the gates of the artistic Yiddish theater to Yiddish folklore, but the same politically slanted approach he had towards the dramatic text was applied to the folklore material.

"The State Theater, as the Soviet inheritor and filter of both the literary classics, and dramatic classics, had to draw from the sparkling sources of the folklore. It does not mean though that he took them unchanged. The Soviet theater could not simply make an inventory of folklore materials. He had to filter and integrate them selectively."[37]

For example Granovsky would take a synagogue tune and put it in a factory scene.

"The Jewish Chamber Theater took upon itself a mission that in other nations was the business of the national opera. It assembled the multitude of musical folklore and processed it into a modern artistic form. The theater thereby fulfilled a very important task; It emancipated the Jewish motif, the Jewish tune, from the dictatorship of the synagogue. Since the synagogue was the center of the old

Jewish life, even secular motifs received a religious infusion. The Chamber Theater returns them to their secular roots. At the same time it also canonizes a whole line of secular street motifs, that never came under the auspices of the synagogue, and had been cause for embarrassment."[38]

## The Tradition of Attacking Tradition

Granovsky strangled the individual characters in their social class. He sacrificed literary content for ideological purposes. Oddly enough the destruction of the Sholem Aleichem character profited not only the revolutionary ideology but also the tool of that ideology, the theater.

Granovsky created a theater of absolute polarity. This made for poor intellectual content and good theater. With Granovsky the colors are brighter, the demarcation lines clearer. The war of the forces of light against the forces of darkness exist in the Bolshevik ideology and in Granovsky's work in the same sharpness and clarity as the Christian theology exists in the Medieval theater. The working class and the bourgeoisie respectively take the place of God and Satan, and the fall of Lucifer-Shimele is this time social.

Granovsky changed the face of the Jewish theater. Paradoxically his defiance of Jewish tradition was genuinely Jewish. Granovsky did not work in a vacuum. He was the *enfant terrible*, but the *enfant terrible* of the Jewish theatre. As Sartre[39] remarked, a Jewish French atheist is not the same as a French atheist. The Jew denies the existence of the Jewish God. The French denies the existence of the Holy Trinity. The two are different because their denial is different. Granovsky did not satirize an abstract society. He satirized the Jewish society. The grotesque imagery of Granovsky was as Jewish as Chagall's fantasy. When the Moscow Jewish State Theater appeared in Berlin, it received a particularly warm write-up from Joseph Roth. In his article Roth related to the conflict between tradition and revolution in the work of the visiting Jewish Theatre.

"This is the childhood disease of the Yiddish theater, and that of the Russian revolution on the whole. The theater remains Jewish even when it attacks Jewish traditions. Attacking the tradition is an old Jewish tradition. I was moved even when they mocked. They mocked, but they mocked in a Jewish way. They were genuine, as genuine as the children of Israel were when Moses smashed the ten commandments."[40]

## *The Jackpot* Under the Direction of Yankev Rotboym

The director Yankev Rotboym[41] was part of the brief golden age of the European Yiddish theater between the two World Wars. He was called upon to direct in The Vilna Troupe [Di Vilner Trupe] when the ensemble found itself in a limbo after the astounding success of The Dybbuk. Rotboym geared the company towards a realistic, socially engaged repertoire. He also directed in another innovative company the Young Theater [Yung Teater] and during World War Two worked in North and South America until he returned to Poland in 1946 where he lived and worked until his death in 1994. Rotboym directed *The Jackpot* in the Polish Jewish State Theater in 1964 and in 1973.

### Rotboym Versus Granovsky

Rotboym knew Granovsky's work. His sister, Lea, was an actress in the Moscow Jewish State Theater. Young Rotboym went to the Soviet Union to see Granovsky's work, including his production of *The Jackpot* which was renamed in Moscow as "200, 000".

Although Rotboym too showed the social conflict in the play, this was not his focus. Rotboym abandoned the sharp class division that marked Granovsky's work. His *Jackpot* is not a play about class struggle within Jewish society, but a Jewish play with a sympathetic attitude towards the characters of the working class. Rotboym used Sholem Aleichem's definition of the play to validate his interpretation: *The Jackpot - A Folk Play in Four Acts. The Jackpot* as Rotboym saw it, was not a revolutionary play but a plebeian one. Rotboym's socialist convictions were reflected in the production: The movement, the dance, the songs emphasized the positive vitality of the working people in their confrontation with the bourgeoisie. Still, after the Granovsky's revolutionary fervor, Rotboym introduced a moderate tone.

## The Characters

Like Granovsky before him Rotboym gave his own interpretation to the play by giving his own interpretation to the characters. Granovsky submerged the individual in his social class. Rotboym rediscovered the individual characters with the social class being but one element of their personalities. Rotboym returned to what was considered an abomination by the revolutionary theater, that is to the psychology of the individual. Naturally, he dealt with the psychology of the characters within the limits allowed by the comedy. He did not turn the text into a psychological drama.

Rotboym relied on guidelines given by Sholem Aleichem himself. Shimele is described as having a beautiful voice. In Rotboym's production he would therefore be a musical tailor, someone who expresses emotions through music. The dream in which a tree with golden coins appears to him in the middle of his poor apartment and foretells his coming fortune, is introduced to the audience by a song. Shimele sings the songs of the golden coins, one of the songs written and composed by Broderson and Kon for Rotboym's first adaptation of the play for The Vilna Troupe in 1931. This song was repeated in seven subsequent adaptations including the production of the Polish Jewish State Theater in 1973.

"Shimele: I hate empty dreams, When I dream there is something to listen to. It's scissors and iron,
Our People! Listen!
I dreamt a dream!
In my dream I'm standing...
I'm standing by my table...
I'm standing and cutting...
Cutting a piece of work with my scissors!

A piece of fine work
Brand new and fresh.
I had a dream
I'm standing in my dream
With scissors in my hand, Exhausted.
I look into the world
I raise my eyes and see
A tree growing in the house.
Beylke: A tree in the middle of the house?
Motl: A tree in the middle of the house?
Kopl: A real tree?
Shimele: And on the tree,
And on the tree
Grow golden coins."[42]

Sholem Aleichem described his play as a "folkplay." Rotboym believed that the infusion of musical numbers into the play was in keeping with the spirit of the Jewish folk theater which was always rich in music and songs.

## The Tailor of the Playwright and the Tailor of the Director

Rotboym saw a connection between Shimele's tendency to drift into a world of fantasy with his incompetence in the real word. In Rotboyms words:

"When Shimele bragged about the quality of this work, you could be sure that the dress was badly cut"[43]

Rotboym, like every director, wrote a secondary text that he superimposed on the original play. It seems though that Rotboym lost sight of the difference between his, and the original text.

"He is a bad tailor but he likes to brag: 'When I start a piece of work!' You can see how bad he is when he measures the suit on Solomontshik. It's too loose, the pants are too long. The waist is too large. You can see by the way they react: 'Oh my God.' You can tell it doesn't fit. It should be say size x and it is size y. I base my interpretation on the text."[44]

The text however does not necessarily imply such an interpretation. According to the text, Shimele can be a poor, or a fine tailor. In my mind Shimele is a good tailor. Rotboym thinks he is a bad one. And we both refer to the same Sholem Aleichem text. Rotboym was not wrong when he said that he based his assumptions on the exact text. This might very well be the case, with one reservation. There is no such thing as the exact text. Every text is made up of words, and the gaps between them that the readers, like nature in medieval physics, rush to fill because they abhor a vacuum.

It seems that the text contains more than one possible interpretation of Shimele's character. I would think that Shimele is a good, artistic tailor. He sings beautifully and is in a way an artist. Sholem Aleichem himself considered artists to be craftsmen and craftsmen to be artists. In his preface to *Stempenyu*[40] he describes writing in terms of craftsmanship. In his correspondence with Berkowitz and the American theater people, Sholem Aleichem liked to use terms from the artisan's world, especially the jargon of the tailors.[45] I can see how the artistic inclination of Shimele would find an outlet in fashioning a garment. Shimele can be a dreamer in his dealing with reality and in the same time a meticulous craftsman when he is doing his job.

With all the reservations one might have about Rotboym's perception of the character, one thing is certain: He created a well defined character. Rotboym's interpretation proved to be a fundamental reaction to Granovsky's attempt to obliterate the individual character from the Jewish theater.

### Rotboym's Music

Both Granovsky and Rotboym added music to the play. But whereas Granovsky had an ideological point, namely the secularization of religious tunes, Rotboym had purely theatrical considerations. Since this comedy was defined by Sholem Aleichem as a "folkplay," the tunes and songs blended in naturally, he thought.

The difference in concept resulted in a difference in the presentation. Granovsky used music to intensify the element of the grotesque. The song about his new name that Shimele Saroker sings after he wins the Jackpot in Granovsky's production makes him look more preposterous. Rotboym used music to make Shimele more endearing. The first thing he buys with his money is a gramophone. The gramophone plays cantorial music, and Shimele hums along with evident pleasure. Rotboym explained:

"Shimele Saroker says Sholem Aleichem, is a Jew 'with a voice.' That is, he is a music lover. He likes to sing. He has a weak spot for singing. In every situation he must express himself in song. At work, when he is happy, and when he wins the money. Later when he is rich he buys himself a gramophone, with records, and a cantor sings. I base my interpretation on a remark by Sholem Aleichem: 'A Jew with a voice.' This was for me the clue that the man is a music lover...If he were not a tailor, he would be an actor, an opera singer. Such tailors later became actors of the Jewish stage."[46]

### The Lyrical Theater After the War

After World War Two, the critical approach to Jewish society, that was typical of the progressive Yiddish theater, changed completely. The attitude towards Jewish life which was exterminated during the war became nostalgic and lyrical. The melodic music of Kon and the poetic text of Broderson lent themselves perfectly to the recreation on stage of the lost *shtetl*.

The songs helped Rotboym maintain the lyrical aspect of Shimele's character despite his new bourgeois status. In contrast to Granovsky, Shimele in Rotboym's production does not try to erase his plebeian past. True, he wants to mingle with his new class, he adopts a Russian name, however he still is the same sympathetic person he used to be. Shimele, in the Sholem Aleichem text, is a mixture of the *nouveau riche* of the European comedy with the Sholem Aleichem folk character.

Rotboym kept both aspects of the character. Rotboym's Shimele remains a *mensch*, a decent human being, even after he becomes rich.

Rotboym emphasized the camaraderie which exists between the former tailor and his ex-apprentices, in spite of the class differences that now divides them. Rotboym repeated the song from the first act about the poverty of the tailors, and constructed a scene wherein all three break out in song and dance.

"Motl: Do you remember, boss!
(sings) Ay ay the poverty cursed be it.
Since it can't hear, it won't do it any harm.
You cannot patch it up,
It creeps in everywhere,
And when you catch it,
It's torn all over. (They dance)
Mendel: (comes in) Sir!
Shimele: What?
Mendel: The guests!
Shimele: They can wait! (goes on dancing)
Mendel: The Feins!
Shimele: The Feins? Tough luck. Well guys, tough luck! Don't forget to say goodbye and come on Saturday! And if my doorman does not let you in, show him who you are! Got it?"[47]

## Rotboym Interprets Eti Meni

"La vraie mesure du théâtre c'est la démesure," commented Ionesco. "The[48] only restraint fit for the theater is the lack of all restraint." Rotboym did not follow this precept. He preferred not to push the comic potential of his characters to the limit. In the margins of the text that served him for his work with The Vilna Troupe in 1931 Rotboym jotted down:

"Careful about Eti Meni: Avoid the comic. She is tired, worried, dramatic. She carries the whole burden on her shoulders."[49]

Granovsky's Eti Meni is a farcical figure. Rotboym went to the other extreme. His Eti Meni is serious. It seems that in his avidity to avoid the grotesque à la Granovsky and to present a positive image of Jewish life, Rotboym did injustice to the sparkling spirit of the Sholem Aleichem comedy.

Rotboym was wrong to assume that Eti Meni could not be comic because she was basically a serious character. Bergson[50] noticed that the funniest animals such as the monkey or the parrot, are in fact the most serious ones. Charlie Chaplin and Buster Keaton knew it. Sholem Aleichem found the comic element in the most down to earth, hard working characters such as the Jewish women in the kitchen and the market place. Eti Meni is certainly one of them. She is funny because she is spiteful. She is perhaps not someone we would like to have to deal with but she is certainly fun to watch on stage. By neutralizing her, Rotboym made her less offensive but also less interesting.

I believe that Rotboym himself knew it. He had his reasons for downgrading the text, and his reasons were not theatrical.

The problem is, in his words:

"How should one present the Jewish type, the Jewish folk type, in a world of increased anti-semitism."[51]

His concern about the image of the Jew on stage increased after the second world war. In a practically *Judenrein* Poland, the Jewish theater is one of the few meeting points between Gentiles and Jews. Out of concern for the image of the Jew, Rotboym got rid of the cursing, and particularly the curses that came out of Eti Meni's mouth. The dialogue between Eti Meni in her new position as a grand dame and the maid reads as follows in Sholem Aleichem's text:

"Eti Meni: The worms should eat you up. You're pretty fresh for a maid.

Yokheved the Maid: (leaves with the keys. Stops for a second) My name is Yokheved!

Eti Meni: Good thing you told me, go to hell Yokheved! (Yokheved leaves. To her husband) What a fresh maid."[52]

Rotboym wrote the following comment in the margins of his book: "Eti Meni curses steadily. She is not sympathetic. (What for?)[53]

Rotboym cut those lines from his text. Without taking up the question of whether the Jewish theater should be committed to presenting a positive image of the Jews, the result is clearly a weaker text.

Taking out the deluge of curses because they showed Eti Meni's evil temper is the same as taking out Tevye's self made commentaries because they show his ignorance. The charm of Eti Meni does not depend on value judgments: Is she a nice person or not. The flowery yiddish curses make the vitality of the character.

Sholem Aleichem's first literary work was a concise alphabetical dictionary of the curses used by his stepmother.[54] In Sholem Aleichem the child, the genius of the artist to come was already apparent: His ability to adopt an amused aesthetic outlook at the harsh reality of Jewish life. Rotboym's approach to the text through rose colored glasses seems irrelevant. He presented a cleaner, but less interesting image of Jewish life. A great deal of the charm of the Jewish folk people lies in the crudeness of the characters. To take out the crudeness is to throw the baby out with the bath water.

## Beylke

Beylke, explains Rotboym, is a girl with willpower, intelligence, self determination. She will not be influenced either by her parents or by the bourgeois society into which she falls after her family becomes rich. Although she is only the daughter of a poor tailor she does not comply with the match with Solomontshik, the son of the town's rich man and elopes instead. In Rotboym's words:

"In those days eloping from home was not a trivial matter. This emphasizes Beylke's strong character".[55]

Rotboym liked the character. He introduced a change in the text so that her positive image would not be damaged.

"The scene in which they draw lots for Beylke. In Sholem Aleichem's play Motl and Beylke decide to cheat Kopl. Do friends act like that? Is this nice? In one word, I avoided it. In my version Beylke herself has to decide. Both of them stand. Both are dear to her. Finally she says: ...But I decided to take...Motl. A very touching scene."[56]

Rotboym cut the original text in which Beylke and Motl plan to defraud Kopl. Rotboym here used the same device that served him in the beginning of the play. A song, this time a romantic song, replaced the rejected text. This way Rotboym kept the lyrical tone of the play.

## Motl and Kopl

Romantic comedies tend to present symmetrically opposed contenders. In *The Two Kuni Leml* Golfaden confronts a handsome student of medicine, with a narrow minded, one eyed Yeshiva student who staggers and limps to boot. In Rotboym's production both Motl and Kopl are handsome, in accordance with the way in which Sholem Aleichem described them.

Apprentices, especially when they come in couples, have been traditionally comic figures. Rotboym, however, decided not to use the comic potential of the two. Instead he emphasized the human side in them, the friendship between them and their kinship to Shimele's household.

In the original text Kopl says that he had a premonition about losing Beylke and therefore bought a ship ticket to America. Rotboym cut this instant solution to Kopl's heartbreak. Instead of delivering the line about leaving, Kopl joins the musicians and accompanies the quiet wedding of Motl and Beylke on his violin.

The emphasis on the sentimental aspect of the characters enhances the romantic tone of the play. Unfortunately, romantic scenes have always been weak spots in comedy, and Sholem Aleichem is no exception. Emphasizing the romantic element meant amplifying the play's weakness rather than its strength.

## Capitalists with Human Faces

There is a theatrical saying that the hat can make the role. Sometimes the actor finds the key to a character through a seemingly insignificant prop. In Granovsky's production Eti Meni looks at the world of the rich through a *pince-nez* made out of two bagels. In Rotboym's production Eti Meni wears a delicate golden one.[57] The same distance that separates Eti Meni in the Granovsky's farce from Eti Meni in Rotboym's social comedy, separates the character of the rich man Fein in the two versions. The prop that visualizes the difference this time is a hat. Rotboym's Mr. Osher Fein wears a small elegant bowler hat, and his suit is in good taste. In the comparison between Granovsky's and Rotboym's work, the difference in the props reveal much about the difference in the interpretations. Rotboym takes off the grotesque masks, and rediscovers the human faces of the Feins. The Feins, as indicated by their name, are the incarnation of fine taste. Rotboym followed Sholem Aleichem, and did not go beyond amused irony in his interpretation of the wealthy man and his wife.

Rotboym relocated the third act. The reception, that serves as Shimele's rite of passage to the rich society, takes place at the Sarokers, and not at the Feins, the way Sholem Aleichem wrote it. In the original play the tailor and his wife come to the house of the Feins filled with awe. In Rotboym's production the old rich bow to the new. The rich man Fein, swallows his pride and comes to Shimele's house in the hope of marrying with the Saroker family.

"In Sholem Aleichem's play Shimele comes to the Feins. I bring the Feins to him. This is a big difference. This way the hypocrisy of the Feins is visible. In the original, Shimele runs to them, and maybe they will do him a favor, and let him in. He becomes cheapened and unsympathetic. In my interpretation the rich become unsympathetic."[58]

For Rotboym, a progressive director, the bourgeoisie is still the enemy, but his interpretation is a far cry from the total war on capitalism declared by Granovsky. The rich man Fein who is but a brush stroke in Garnovsky's picture of the bourgeois society, regains a human face under Rotboym's direction. An actor (Szymon Szurmiej) who fell sick helped inadvertently in shaping the part.

"With Szymon I had an interesting story. I always presented Fein like a high class person who has a lot of money and eats very well. And all the actors were such fat looking Jews. I always had a hard time getting Szymon to rehearsals. He is the head of the theater. I give him a role and he gives me a hard time. Once when he did not show up for the rehearsal, I went to his office. He said to me: Oy I have got a cold, oy I can't walk, it hurts here...I said to him: Play Fein the way you are! Fein can be sick. He said: What do you mean sick?! I say: The same way you are sick now, he will be sick. I dragged him to the stage, gave him a cane, and he came on stage this way (Rotboym demonstrates by walking bent, leaning heavily on the stick, and sitting down with a heavy sigh.) Today he plays this way. In perfect health he plays a sick man. It is very interesting. The idea came from an incident. A rich man has a million dollars but he has a sick stomach, a weak heart."[59]

Although a communist himself, Rotboym's style was a reaction to the black and white picture presented in the Soviet theater.

"This is how one should play the enemy. Not openly. The enemy is dangerous because one cannot recognize him! Nature shows us how serpents or birds take on the color of the trees so they will not be recognized. So this shows you how false it is when the wealthy man looks one hundred percent wealthy. Szymon's sickly wealthy man who is scarcely alive is more real than the wealthy man with the healthy bass voice. Even though he is on the verge of death, he still wants to finagle the hundred thousand for his son, Solomontshik."[60]

Rotboym's sick rich man is a sick individual and at the same time he is the representative of a sick social class. Granovsky used the grotesque style to convey ideological messages. Rotboym shows that a realistic approach can be ideologically charged too.

"At the same time he is a symbol of a sick social class. This is not a play about class struggle. Sholem Aleichem did not write about class struggle. But it is a plebeian play. This you will find in my interpretation."[61]

## Solomontshik Fein

Rotboym rediscovered the individual characters not only in his interpretation of the key characters but also in the secondary roles such as Solomontshik, Osher Fein's son.

Solomontshik represents the young generation of the Jewish bourgeoisie. Sholem Aleichem made fun of the cultural emptiness and assimilation of the young rich Jews of his time. The Yiddish that he put in Solomontshik's mouth was bastardized and Russified. His language goes hand and hand with his appearance. His dress is very European: he wears elegant casual summer suits and French straw hats.

Rotboym returned to the Stanislavsky method and its psychological build up of the character. Rotboym instructed the actor to imagine the whole personality of the individual he is going to portray:

"Solomontshik went to a Russian school. He speaks Russian. He hangs around with students, and with rich people. He eventually plays billiards or cards. He has many female acquaintances. He strolls around, he gets drunk. If you play the role of Solomontshik you will have to make up his biography. Imagine what do you do, being a son of such a family. Why is it that you order a suit in Shimele's shop? Because he lives in the house and does not pay rent. So your father says: He doesn't pay the rent let him at least sew a garment. I assume that Fein is stingy. If he had to pay for it, he would pick another tailor. After this comes a very beautiful girl, Beylke, and he lusts after her. One more girl? Why not? She is poor, her father does not pay the rent, maybe he can take advantage of her."[62]

Rotboym came a long way from the anti-psychological theater of Granovsky. Under his direction, complex characters replaced Granovsky's social masks.

## The Society Women

Granovsky used the society ladies as spots of color on a giant grotesque picture. Rotboym tried to give an individual touch to each character.

"The irony of the society ladies. They say about the Sarokers who won the lottery: 'You don't have to be smart, all it takes is luck.' In my production the ladies are not caricatures as in Granovsky's interpretation. He made a caricature out of them. In my performance they are people."[62]

Rotboym gave minute attention to every single character:

"Madame Fein's first sentence says who she is. 'You don't have to be beautiful, you don't have to be smart, you need a little luck. That's all. My husband has millions of lottery tickets, and with all due respect, this little tailor has no more than one ticket. I could lose my mind'. She cannot wish him well. This is the antagonism between the two social classes. If another person would have won the Jackpot, someone from her circle, she would not begrudge him. In her mind Shimele does not have the right to win."[63]

Rotboym drew a detailed picture even of the smallest roles. He added text to characters who had none in the original play. He wanted to give each actor and actress the minimum necessary to create an individual role.

"I have a principle. If an actor is on stage, he should have something to say. Because otherwise he is not interested. 'I have nothing to say anyway...' Either Madame Koltun agrees with Madame Fein, or she is against her. As the wife of Koltun she is dependent on Madame Fein, because Koltun is their employee. 'It goes without saying, since you say so...' Or she can be a miniature of a society lady. She sits with the rest of them in a café and listens to the latest gossip. It depends how you want to present the role."[64]

## Mr. and Mrs. Koltun

When he said that he added his own text to Madame Koltun, it was an understatement. In fact it would be more accurate to say that Rotboym added a character that did not exist in the original text at all: Madame Koltun. Furthermore, in the original play the celibacy of Koltun is part of his character. Koltun is one of the men who want Beylke. Rotboym did not like it. He turned him from an elderly bachelor to a respectable family man with a belly and a fancy walking cane, and his wife joined the ladies who giggle in approval at Madame Fein's venomous remarks. By introducing this change, explained Rotboym, he achieved two goals: He enlarged the social circle around the Feins, and eliminated Koltun as a romantic partner for Beylke. When Koltun courted Beylke it made her look cheap, and interfered with the lyrical atmosphere he wanted to give to the play. In Rotboym's words:

"Koltun is not an old bachelor in my play, because if an old bachelor tries to marry her, what is she anyway? A whore that everybody wants to touch? Alright, the two young men, or Solomontshik, but an old bachelor, this is very ugly."[65]

Rotboym could give Koltun a more complex, less negative interpretation, but then the character would acquire tragic dimensions, and drift too far away from the comic orbit. In his words:

"Or he must be a tragic character, who knows that only a poor girl would fall for him because she has no dowry and he will do her a favor. Then one has to play the role altogether differently, and we step out of comedy. Koltun becomes a tragic figure. It wouldn't be the same thing. You could do it. It doesn't pay. You have to decide what is more important. If you go today from here to Warsaw, you do not want to end up in Berlin, but in Warsaw. Because Berlin is in the exact opposite direction. You have to know which way you are going. You buy a ticket, you inquire at what time the train departs. You calculate the time. You have a whole plan, and entire composition that you have to consider if you want to get to Warsaw. How do you present the play? What do you want to get out of the play? What is the main idea?"[66]

## Soloveitchik

The names are significant in Sholem Aleichem's drama. Koltun means a sickness of the scalp. Soloveitchik means a little nightingale. Rotboym embellished the characters in order to keep the lyrical mood of the performance. Unpleasant features underwent a sort of plastic surgery . Koltun loses the repulsive physical characteristics implied by his name and becomes a respectable member of the local petty bourgeoisie. Soloveitchik who like the pet bird must please everyone, gets a less satirical, more sympathetic treatment from Rotboym. In Rotboym's interpretation, the wheeling dealing matchmaker hides a delicate soul. Soloveitchik feels Shimele's pain after the loss of the money. He is the only guest at the party who remains with Shimele after the bad news arrive. Without sacrificing the comic element of the hyper, endlessly lobbying, meddling matchmaker, Rotboym gave him psychological depth:

"I established a hierarchy: Who is sympathetic and who is not. Soloveitchik is one of the sympathetic characters. He is a tragic figure. He can marry off all the daughters, except his own. Sholem Aleichem wrote a story: 'Nisht Gefidlt.' In this story he wrote about matchmakers with certain sadness. The shoemakers go barefoot and the matchmakers make matches for others, because they do not have a dowry for their own daughters. But on the outside, Soloveitchik is full of optimism. He is elegant. He has no right to be sad. He must be the symbol of optimism. He is a sympathetic man...When the bank clerk tells everybody that Shimele lost his money, they all rejoice, they laugh. Soloveitchik feels for Shimele and stays with him. He wants to comfort him. He helps to look for the daughter. In the final scene he is there as a friend of the family. He is not a stranger."[67]

Rotboym changed the traditional image of the matchmaker in the Yiddish theater. The matchmaker in the Jewish theater was traditionally an erratic character. He was continually in a sweat, running all over the place, a red handkerchief hanging from his pocket, hopelessly trying to make a living. Rotboym suggested a new interpretation of the character. He referred to Sholem Aleichem's description of the character: "Soloveitchik: a modern matchmaker with bowler hat."[68] Rotboym made the matchmaker more modern and sophisticated.

"Soloveitchik: 'A modern matchmaker' What does modern mean in that context? In the Jewish plays the matchmaker is a sort of good for nothing. He has a split goatee. One half for the brides's side and one side for the groom. He can bring two walls together. He tries every trick in the book! 'A modern matchmaker with a bowler hat!' That means that he comes and goes in the rich houses, he always finds a way. He has some sophistication. When they dance, Soloveitchik leads them. In those days you had a person who was master of ceremonies at the dances. He is a man of the world. He has manners. Everything about him is comical and yet he fits himself in among the rich."[69]

Thus, the ball scene serves a completely different purpose in Rotboym's and in Granovsky's productions. Granovsky made of it a biting satire. Rotboym used it to deepen his psychological interpretation of the characters.

## Vigdortchuk and Robintchik

The two con men who rob Shimele of his money both come from professions related to the theater. One is an ex-musician, and the other a wig maker. They have an artistic predisposition to create make believe. They lure Shimele to invest money in their movie theater ventures. They convince him in a scene where they charm him by speaking about the magic of the movies. Then they run away with his money.

Fraud scenes have always held a rich potential for comedy. They are very theatrical. A good example for a fraud scene is the one in which Mosieur Jourdain is fooled by the phoney Sultan of Turkey in the *Bourgeois Gentleman*. In the impersonation scenes the theater rediscovers for a moment the joyful synthesis between playing as in acting and playing as in fun and games. It is particularly surprising therefore that Rotboym chose to cut the fraud scene complete with the two charlatans who perform it.

Peter Frei who directed the play in the Tel-Aviv Ohel Theater, knew the original Sholem Aleichem text and yet used the Berkowitz version which omitted the fraud scene completely. Frei made this choice for dramatic reasons. The fraud scene is almost half an hour long, and opens a kind of a play within a play. This slows down the rhythm of the performance as a whole. Frei thought that the two characters were too flat, and did not justify the attention Sholem Aleichem gave them. In Frei's words:

"It seems to me that Berkowitz's version was more accomplished. He opened and closed in a smaller circle than Sholem Aleichem, but accomplished thereby a certain perfection. Whereas in Sholem Aleichem's original play, the entrance of those two good for nothings who sell him on the idea of silent movies, of film making, suddenly starts a new play, out of the blue. I find this arbitrary. Furthermore those characters are stereotypical and flat. The character of Shimele is well founded, with deep roots, like the people who surround him, Eti Meni, the daughter, the two apprentices, all the townspeople. They are all whole characters, extraordinary characters. In contrast, the two con men make their entrance towards the end, for a short while, and somehow it is less convincing. Maybe I was wrong. Somehow after comparing Sholem Aleichem and Berkowitz, I decided to stick with Berkowitz"[70]

Rotboym like Frei, had theatrical reasons for omitting the scene. Faithful to the concept of what he called a plebeian play, Rotboym added music, songs and dance. Cutting out the scene with the scoundrels left space for all that.

"Since I wanted to make a musical comedy, it would have come out too long. I had to make place for the songs. I had to cut out unnecessary things. You can mention the business with Vigdortchuk and Rubintchik without actively presenting it. A spectator who didn't read the play does not feel that it is missing."[71]

Unlike Frei, Rotboym's approach to the scene was not purely theatrical. His motivation was basically emotional, and Rotboym was the first to admit it. In the text that served him for the production with The Vilna Troupe in 1931, he encircled the whole scene with large question marks, and decided to omit the scene completely. He reintroduced the scene in his production in the Folksbine in 1943 in New York, but subsequently omitted it from the four productions he directed thereafter. The reservation Rotboym had about the two characters was moral, not theatrical: They personified cheating and fraud. These were not characters that Rotboym was keen to present in the anti-semitic Europe before World War Two, let alone after it. The two con men were too out of line with the lyrical image Rotboym wanted to create on stage.

"They are not professionals. Absolute con men. Ugly types. What do I need them for? And Shimele looks and believes them. He likes it. The audience gets the message: A Jew is a swindler. Especially after the war, here in Poland, the audience is eighty per cent non-Jewish, or in Germany. Jews do not want to see ugly Jews on stage either."[72]

## The Lyrical Theater After the War

The progressive Jewish Theater before World War II was characterized by sharp social critique. After the war the criticism subsided. This change was not limited to Poland. The approach of the theater to the Jewish society which was destroyed during the war became a loving one, and the tone turned lyrical. Rotboym said about this change:

"It is a problem: How to present the Jew in a world of intensified anti-semitism. I would have done it differently before Hitler. A lot sharper. And today I do it differently. In the Folksbine production of 1943, Solomontchik looks like a clown. After the war he was fashionable, nicely dressed. I try while directing Jewish plays to present the Jew in a delicate way, not idealizing him, presenting him as an angel, but I would never direct Ash's *God of Vengeance* today. I would not do it for all the money in the world."[73]

In *God of Vengeance* a wealthy Jewish brothel keeper finds a respectable match for his daughter, but she instead becomes a whore.

## Rotboym and the Critics

The critics' reviews reflect the changes in Rotboym's work. The production with the Folksbine in 1943 in New York was typical of the progressive Jewish theater in the years between the two world wars. Granovsky's influence was very deeply felt in the production. The Sholem Aleichem text served as a spring board for the theater of the grotesque and for the use of avant-garde theatrical techniques such as contructivist stage design. The critic in the foreword wrote:

"Sholem Aleichem's comedy, *The Jackpot* changed in the Folksbine from the previous productions. The director, Yankev Rotboym, introduced into the play the spirit of the grotesque, and changed it into a very light folk play which takes place somewhere in the air, in some fantastic world, not on earth. Sholem Aleichem reveals himself in a modernistic version, with various new stage devices, which are, by the way, not very new, because they were used quite often in the last years. We see here on the stage platforms, stairs, ladders, and other theatrical devices which were very much in vogue in the theatrical world for a while."[74]

The caricature-like characters of Vigdortchuk and Robintchik fit into Rotboym's grotesque interpretation of the play. Their performances attracted the attention of the critics.

"The two shrewd Jews, the swindlers, Vigdortchuk and Robintchik, are portrayed in a light grotesque way by Yankev Rosenblum, and Baruch Fayvelovitsh."[75]

In his work in Warsaw in 1964, the two swindlers were gone.

In a detailed review, the critic D. Ginzberg analyzed the two tendencies that characterized Rotboym's later interpretation of the play. On the one hand Rotboym could not set himself free from the influence of the man who shaped his artistic concepts: Alexander Granovsky. Granovsky's perfect visual compositions seduced and enchanted Rotboym, who was also a painter. Rotboym followed his master and organized the stage into one unified composition.

"Yankev Rotboym has in his interpretation to this day elements from Granovsky and Meyerhold. On top of that, he is a painter himself. He draws the characters on paper with all their details. He is a master of the *mise en scène*. He sees the stage with the eyes of a painter: It has to be composed properly, get a touch of paint here and a spot of paint there."[76]

But Ginzberg claimed that Rotboym created a somewhat distorted picture. He wanted to be lyrical but did not know how:

"Rotboym has a way of sharpening, he is better at catching the heavy, the depressing rather than at catching the soft, lyrical, delicate, silky elements."[77]

The audience was assaulted with comedy, melodrama, light opera and even vaudeville. Although the proficiency of the director was felt in each sequence, an overall concept of the play was missing.

"With all the theatrical qualities of the play, it still lacked something. The director used various artistic devices, but failed to create a style of his own. Vaudeville, opera, melodrama, comedy - yes, but put together, what does it amount to?"[78]

The critic thought that the production had many shapes and colors, but no soul.

"Too many theatrical devices, too many mechanical means replaced the simple, human, plain hearty and wise smile of Sholem Aleichem. One can feel the ambitious spirit behind the performance. It would have been perhaps better to have less ambition and more of Sholem Aleichem. Rotboym has too much experience in the theater, too much directorial know-how, to keep a critic from telling him all that openly."[79]

The Polish Jewish Theater travelled a lot. *The Jackpot* was performed by the theater in 1971 in Switzerland. The critic of the National Basler Zeitung devoted a highly insightful article to the performance. The writer himself was aware of the irony in his criticism. He found the theatrical style of the director to be completely archaic. The critic who displayed an astonishing knowledge of the history of the Yiddish theater, could not find an explanation for such an obsolete interpretation from a director of Rotboym's background and stature. The critic, in his pain, tried to find plausible explanations that ranged from the senile state of the director, to the nostalgic mood in the post-war Jewish theater. He came, with a tone of sadness, to the conclusion that the tradition of the Jewish theater in Eastern Europe had in fact died. The living theater had been amputated. What was left were museum pieces subsidized by the state. In his words:

"An old, archaically stylized theater was offered to us. This is surprising from a director of the likes of Rotboym, who originally won recognition by staging Brecht, and who belonged to the progressive wing of the Jewish theater before the war. He began in the famous Vilna Troupe. He then worked with Michael Weichert, the highly interesting Polish-Jewish director of the period between the two world wars whose Young Theater [Yung Teater] could be compared only to Art et Action or to the theatrical laboratory of Louise Lara in Paris. Weichert was interested in the creation of a new versatile stage space, and in new spontaneous performance techniques rather than in experimenting with the written text. Did Rotboym forget everything he saw and did there? One would prefer to think that this is not a reactionary setback, but rather a nostalgic resignation! The once thriving Jewish theater in Poland was as good as wiped out by the Nazi extermination and the political post war developments. The only possible remainder is a shadow of its former self."[80]

## *The Jackpot* - Epilogue

The successive eras of the Yiddish theater from the thirties to the eighties are reflected in Rotboym'swork.

His interpretation to *The Jackpot* went from the daring grotesque to a lyrical realism after the war. The Yiddish theater in Europe resembles a film that came to an end yet keeps on running - backwards. This reverse chronology is reflected in Rotboym's work. His *Jackpot* of the forties is far more daring and innovative than his works in the eighties. Itsik Manger[81] wrote a poem about a mother who wraps her beloved child to protect him against the winter cold. The many layers of clothes are too heavy. The child who wanted to be a bird cannot fly, because of his mother's love.

The Yiddish theater after the Second World War was carefully protected by the surviving directors. The idea was to take loving care of what was left. There is no room for a Granovsky in the Yiddish theater today. Aggression, spite, care free humor and biting satire - in other words the stuff good theater is made of - are all banned. Rotboym was part of this trend and his case is particularly striking. His later work seems to be a reaction to his own, early achievements.

# 7. Epilogue

Sholem Aleichem foresaw the creation of a Yiddish artistic theater, but did not live to be part of it. His plays, which were shunned by the theater during his life time, became the classic repertoire of the Yiddish Theater after his death.

From Sholem Aleichem's pen came brilliant dialogues, authentic pictures of Jewish life, and unforgettable stage characters.

It has been said that *The Treasure* is made of a series of images, which beautiful in themselves, fail to create a unified play. However, the Russian director, Dicky, made a theatrical gem out of it.

Although the main event (Hava's interfaith marriage) happens off stage, and Tevye, in defiance of dramatic rules, talks a lot and acts little, the play became a classic of the Jewish theater.

The plot in *The Jackpot* is simple, still the play became a central piece of the progressive Jewish theater between the two world wars. It was performed repeatedly, and its characters and their sayings became national folklore. It is one of the most popular Jewish comedies to this day.

Sholem Aleichem never directed any of his plays. He was not given the opportunity to perfect them in the theater. This assignment was left to subsequent directors who became paramount figures in the realization of Sholem Aleichem's drama on stage.

Meyerhold, in an article entitled "First Attempt at a Stylized Theater"[1] distinguished between two kinds of directors:

"The two methods may be explained by illustrating the four basic theatrical elements (Author, Director, Actor, Spectator) as follows:

1. A triangle, in which the apex is the director and the two remaining corners, the author and the actor. The spectator comprehends the creation of the latter two through the creation of the director. This is method one, which we shall call the Theater Triangle:

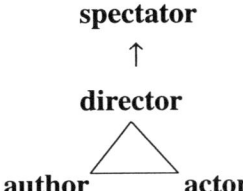

2. A straight, horizontal line with the four theatrical elements (Author, Director, Actor, Spectator) marked from left to right represents the other method, which we shall call, 'The Theater of the Straight Line'. The Actor reveals his soul freely to the spectator, having assimilated the creation of the director, who in turn, has assimilated the creation of the author:

author → director → actor → spectator

The two major comedies of Sholem Aleichem, *The Jackpot* and *The Treasure* went through the two models of Meyerhold. Granovsky and Dicky were directors of the triangular theater. Both squeezed the actors into well defined molds. *The Jackpot* in the Moscow Jewish State Theater was first and foremost the encounter between Granovsky and the audience. *The Treasure* in Habima was mainly the encounter of the audience with Dicky. Granovsky held the text and the actors in the grip of his grotesque hyperboles. Although Dicky left the actors more room for individual acting, he too imposed strict constraints. Heavy make up, highly stylized costumes, and tightly orchestrated mass scenes emphasized the presence of the director. Granovsky and Dicky were both Soviet directors of the first years after the Revolution. Their interpretations were daring, expressive, and sharp.

Rotboym and Berger are, on the other hand, directors of what Meyerhold called "The Theater of the Straight Line." They treat the text with more respect. Unlike Dicky who did not speak Yiddish, or Granovsky who felt more at ease in Russian, Both Rotboym and Berger speak Yiddish, and know Sholem Aleichem's work. Rotboym and Berger let the text, and thereby the actor, speak for themselves. The encounter here is between the spectator and the actor.

The ideological zeal that characterized the generation of the founders (with the exception of Maurice Schwartz) gave way to restraint. Along with this, came a return to theatrical conservatism.

The emergence of new generations of directors cut off from the historical Eastern European Jewish way of life, that is from the soil and roots of Sholem Aleichem's creation, confronts the Jewish theater with a new problem. A barrier of language and culture now separates them from the original works of Sholem Aleichem.

Paradoxically this very alienation can bring about a renewed interest in the historical and cultural background of Sholem Aleichem's drama.

But the return to old content, cannot be followed by a return to the old theatrical style. In Bunim's words:

"One has to play in allusion, understating, stylizing. You have to project the Sholem Aleichem material with its deep human and Jewish content, in a modern way. Otherwise it will not reach the public and remain a chapter in the history of the theater".[2]

The theater has to keep looking for new theatrical forms, without losing the soul of the Sholem Aleichem text. Future directors will have to find a new pitcher for the old Sholem Aleichem wine.

# NOTES

The translation of Yiddish and Hebrew texts unless not indicated otherwise were done by the author.

## 1. The Life of Sholem Aleichem

1. *Sholem Aleichem, Funem Yarid* in *Ale Verk Fun Sholem Aleichem [From The Fair* in *Complete works of Sholem Aleichem] Vol 26-27* (New York: Foksfond Oysgagbe 1923).
   Translated by Curt Leviant as *From The Fair* (New York: Viking Penguin Inc. 1985). Hereafter referred to as *Funem Yarid*.

2. *Di Yidishe Folksbibliotek [The Jewish Folk Library]*, Kiev, 1888. Hereafter referred to as *Folksbibliotek*.

3. *YOKENHOZ Oder dos Groyse Berzenshpil - A Komedie in Fir Aktn*, in *Ale Verk fun Sholem Aleichem*, Volume 24 - *Komedyes [YOKENHOZ Or The Great Stock Exchange Gamble -* in *Complete Works of Sholem Aleichem*, Vol. 24 - *Comedies]* (New York: Folksfond 1923) 29-134. Volume 24 will hereafter be referred to as : *Komedyes*.

4. All the Tevye monologues are included in the first volume of *Ale Verk fun Sholem Aleichem* [Complete Works of Sholem Aleichem] entitled *Gants Tevye der Milkhiker [All Tevye The Dairyman]* (New York: Sholem Aleichem Folksfond Oysgabe 1927). Hereafter referred to as: *Gants Tevye der Milkhiker*.
   Frances Butwin's *Tevye's Daughters* (New York: Crown publishers, 1949) includes only four of the monologues (*Hodl, Hava, Shprintse* and *Tevye Goes to Palestine*).

5. *Tsezeyt un Tseshpreyt [Scattered and Dispersed]*, in *Ale Verk fun Sholem Aleichem [Complete Works of Sholem Aleichem]*, volume 4, *Dramatishe Shriftn [Dramatic Works]* (New York: Morgen Frayhayt, 1923) 41-98.
There is no English translation of the play.

6. There is no English translation of the play.

7. *Dos Sholem Aleichem Bukh [The Sholem Aleichem Book]* edited by I. D. Berkowitz (New York: Sholem Aleichem Bukh-Komitet 1926) 62. Hereafter referred to as *Dos Sholem Aleichem Bukh*.

8. Berkowitz, I. D. *Harishonim Kivney Adam [The Pioneers as Private People]* (Tel Aviv: Dvir, 1959). Hereafter referred to as *Harishonim*.

9. *Yidishe tekhter oder Stempenyu - A drame in fir aktn un dray bilder fun Sholem Aleichem*. Eygentum des hern Boris Thomashefsky. [*Jewish Daughters or Stempenyu - A Drama In Four Acts And Three Sceneries*. Property of Mister Tomashefsky].
The text was copied in script letters by B. Kammer who added his signature and the date: February 3, 1907. The manuscript is kept in the YIVO archive in New York. Hereafter referred to as *The YIVO manuscript*.

10. *Der Oytser [The Treasure]*. The manuscript is kept in Bet Shalom Aleichem in Tel Aviv. Later entitled as *Di Goldgreber [The Gold Diggers]* in <u>Di Zukunft</u> (New York: 1927, October, November, December issues) 555-568, 618-623, 682-687.
The play was not included in *Ale Verk fun Sholem Aleichem [Complete Works of Sholem Aleichem]*. There is no English translation of the play. Hereafter referred to as *Di Goldgreber*.

11. Sholem Aleichem, *Dos Groyse Gevins [The Jackpot]*. The play was published in *Di Zukunft* (New York: 1916) February - March issues.
*Dos Groyse Gevins* was included in *Dramatishe Shriftn* in *Ale Verk fun Sholem Aleichem [The Jackpot in Dramatic Works in Complete Works Of Sholem Aleichem]* (New York: Folksfond 1917) Vol. 4 Pages 151-256. Hereafter referred to as: *Dos Groyse Gevins*.
The Jackpot is the only major Sholem Aleichem play available in English translation.

*The Jackpot - A Folk Play In Four Acts*, Trans. by Kobi Weitzner and Barnett Zumoff (New York: The Workmen's Circle Educating Department, 1989). Hereafter referred to as *The Jackpot.*

## 2. From Page to Stage

1. Aristotle, *On The Art Of Poetry* in *Aristotle Horace Lnoginus -Classical Literary Criticism* Trans. by T. S. Dorsch (Harmondsworth: Penguin Classics, 1969) 29-76.

2. Zylbercweig, Zalmen. *Lexikon fun yidishn teater* (*Lexicon Of The Yiddish Theater*), *Vol* 4 (New York: Farlag Elisheva, 1963) 3431-3432. Hereafter referred to as *Lexicon.*

## 3. Stempenyu

1. Sholem Aleichem, *Shomer's mishpet oder der sud prisyazhnik oyf ale romanen fun shomer stenografirt vort am vort durkh Sholem Aleichem* [*The Trial of Shomer or All The Novels of Shomer Brought Before the Jury. Meticulously stenographed by Sholem Aleichem*] (Berdichev: Sheftl, 1888).

2. *Stempenyu*, Trans by H. Berman (London: Methuen and co. 1913). The Yiddish novel is included in Vol. 11 entitled *Yidishe Romanen* in *Ale verk fun Sholem Aleichem* [*Jewish Love Stories* in *Complete Works of Sholem Aleichem*] (New York: Folksfond, 1923).

3. Wolfson Aaron, *Leichtsin und Fromelei - ein Familiengemälde in drei Aufzüge von Wolfson* in *Lustspiele zur Unterhaltung beim Purimfeste* [*Frivolity and Bigotry - A Family Portrait in Three Acts for Entertainment on Purim Holiday*] (Breslau: Königliche Preußische Stadt Brandtdruckerei, 1796) 33-111.

4. *Lexicon* 3343.

5. The letter dated April Tenth 1903 is kept in Bet Shalom Aleichem archives in Tel Aviv.

6. *Dos Sholem Aleichem Bukh* 209.

7. The YIVO manuscript.

8. Sholem Aleichem, *Stempenyu* in *Di yidishe folksbibliotek* [*The Jewish Folk Library*] (Kiev: 1888) 4. Hereafter referred to as *Stempenyu - The Novel*.

9. The YIVO manuscript 13.

10. Ibid 21.

11. Ibid 21.

12. *Stempenyu - The Novel* 24.

13. Luckacz F. L. *Tragedy - Serious Drama in Relation to Aristotle's Poetics* (London: Chatto and Windus, 1957) 94-95.

14. The Yivo manuscript 77.

15. Ibid 83.

16. Ibid 83.

17. Rumshinsky Yosef, *Klangn fun mayn lebn* [*Sounds Of My Life*] (New York: Farlag A. I. Biderman, 1944) 310.

18. Niger Shmuel, *Vegn yidishe shrayber: kritishe artiklen* [*About Yiddish Writers: Critical Essays*] (Warsaw Vilnius, 1913) Vol 1 page 73.

19. Sholem Aleichem's introduction to *Stempenyu* in *Di yidishe folksbibliotek*.

20. Mendele Moykher Sforim, *Der priziv: a drame in finf aktn gedrukt behisshadles Mendele Moykher Sforim* [*The Recruitment: A Drama in Five Acts printed by Mendele Moykher Sforim*] (St. Petersburg: I. Cederboym, 1885).

21. Itsik Manger wrote about the dramatic potential of his *Megile Lider* [*Megile Songs*] in the preface to his *Hotsmakh shpil* [*Hotsmakh Play*] (London: Farlag Aleyninyu, 1947).

22. Interview with Shmuel Bunim in café Roval, December 10, 1978 in Tel Aviv. I keep a recording and gave a transcript of this interview, like all the other interviews I conducted for this book, to the Institute

of Oral History at the Hebrew University in Jerusalem. Hereafter referred to as Interview with Bunim.

23. The YIVO manuscript 33.

24. Ibid 82.

25. *Stempenyu* adapted by Shmuel Bunim and Yaakov Shabtay (Tel Aviv, 1972) 94-95. The play was never published and it is kept in the Habima archive in Tel Aviv, hereafter referred to as *Stempenyu - The Prompt Book*.

26. Manger Itsik, *Megile Lider [Megile Songs]* (Tel Aviv: Amikam, 1976). This is Manger's poetic rendition of the biblical *Book Of Ester*.

27. Manger Itsik, *Midrash Itsik* (Jerusalem: The Yiddish Department at the Hebrew University in Jerusalem, 1969).

28. *Stempenyu - The Prompt Book* 84.

29. Sholem Aleichem, "Baym Keynig Akhashveyrosh" in *Mayses far yidishe kinder: Tsveytes bukh* Vol. 4 of *Ale Verk fun Sholem Aleichem*. ["At The House Of King Ahasuerus" in *Stories for Jewish Children: Second Book* in Vol. 4 of *Complete Works of Sholem Aleichem*] (New York: Folksfond 1927) 53.

30. *Stempenyu - The Prompt Book* 63.

31. *Bay Unds Yidn [Among Us Jews]*, edited by I. Vonvild (Warsaw: Di Velt, 1923) 154.

32. Halevy Shoshana,"Purimshpil bitsfat milifney 90 shana" ["Purim Play in Safed 90 Years Ago"] in *Yeda Am (Jerusalem 1967) vol. 31-32, page 50-55.*

33. *Stempenyu - The Prompt Book* 61-63.

34. *Ibid 64-65.*

35. *Stempenyu - The Novel 6-7.*

36. Sholem Aleichem, *Moshkele Ganev* [*Moshkele The Thief*] (Warsaw: Familien Bibliotek, 1913).

37. *Stempenyu* trans by I. D. Berkowitz, in Vol. 13 of *Kitvey Shalom Aleichem* [*Works of Shalom Aleichem*] (Tel Aviv: Devir, 1941).

38. Interview with Bunim.

39. "Audiences enjoys *Stempenyu* hugely" in The New York Times (New York, March 3rd 1929).

40. Ben Ami Nachman, "Sipur shel Ahava - *Stempenyu* beteatron 'Habima'" ["A Love Story - *Stempenyu* In The Habima Theater"] in Maariv (Tel Aviv, April 4th, 1972).

41. Ibid.

42. Ibid.

43. Zartal Idit, "Havay kalush" ["Diluted Folklore"] in Davar (Tel Aviv, April 12th 1972).

44. Ibid.

45. Ibid.

46. Ibid.

47. Evron Boaz, "Schmaltz bemirvakh meshaashea" ["Entertaining Schmaltz"] in Yediot Akhronot (Tel Aviv, April 9th 1972).

48. Ibid.

49. *Dos Sholem Aleichem Bukh* [*The Sholem Aleichem Book*] 61.

## 4. The Treasure

1. Sholem Aleichem, *Haotsar* in *Shalom Aleichem: Ketavim Ivriyim*, [*The Treasure* in *Sholem Aleichem*: *Hebrew Works*] (Tel Aviv: Bet Shalom Aleichem 1976) 107.

2. Pascal Blaise, *The Pensées,* Trans. by J. M. Cohen (Penguin Books: 1961) 164.

3. The letter is kept in *Bet Shalom Aleichem* in Tel Aviv.

4. *Harishonim* [*The Pioneers*]163.

5. Ibid. 167.

6. *Di Goldgreber* [*The Gold Diggers*].

7. Shalom Aleichem *Haotsar* in Vol. 6 of *Kol Kitvey Shalom Aleichem - Komediot* [*The Treasure in Complete Works of Sholem Aleichem - Comedies*] (Tel Aviv: Dvir 1929) . Hereafter referred to as: *Haotsar [The Treasure].*

8. *Harishonim* [*The Pioneers*] 178.

9. Peretz I. L., *In Polish oyf der Keyt* in <u>Literarishe Monatsshriftn</u> *[In The Synagogue Anteroom* in <u>Literary Monthly</u>] (February 1908) 18-30.
The magazine published only the first act of the play. Hereafter referred to as: *In polish oyf der keyt.*

10. Manuscript of the third version of *The Treasure* 4-5. The Manuscript is kept in Bet Shalom Aleichem in Tel Aviv. Hereafter referred to as: Third version.

11. *In polish oyf der keyt* [In *The Synagogue Anteroom*] 18.

12. Ibid. 22.

13. The letter from March 21st 1908 is kept in Bet Shalom Aleichem in Tel Aviv.

14. The letter is kept in Bet Shalom Aleichem in Tel Aviv.

15. *Haotsar* [*The Treasure*] 3.

16. Ibid. 47.

17. Ibid. The Preface.

18. Gorchakov A. Nikolai *The Theater in Soviet Russia* (New York: Books for Libraries Press, 1972). Hereafter referred to as: *The Theater in Soviet Russia*.

19. *Max Reinhardt und Sein Theater in Bildern* [*Max Reinhardt and his Theater in Picture*] (Salzburg: Max Reinhardt Forschungstätte, 1968).

20. I interviewed the actor Shmuel Rodensky in café Ugati in Tel Aviv on December 26th 1980. Hereafter referred to as: Interview with Rodensky.

21. Dicky's prompt book of *The Treasure* from the Habima production in 1928, page 7. The prompt book is kept in the Habima archives in Tel Aviv. Hereafter referred to as: Dicky's prompt book.

22. Ibid. 10.

23. Ibid. 22.

24. Ibid. 23.

25. I interviewed the actress Hanale Händler at her home in Tel Aviv on December 16th, 1980. Hereafter referred to as: Interview with Hanale Händler.

26. I interviewed the actor Rafael Klatchkin at his home in Tel Aviv on December 12th, 1980. Hereafter referred to as: Interview with Rafael Klatchkin.

27. Ibid.

28. The program of *The Treasure* in the Polish Jewish State Theater (Warsaw: June 1969). Hereafter referred to as: The program of *The Treasure*.

29. Sholem Aleichem *Mazel Tov* in *Komedyes* 140.

30. I interviewed the actor Juliusz Berger at his jome in Warsaw on April 10th, 1979. Hereafter referred to as: Interview with Berger.

31. The prompt book of *The Treasure* adapted by Chewel Buzgan and Moyshe Szwejlich. (Warsaw: 1969) 25-26. The prompt book is kept in the archives of the Polish Jewish State Theater in Warsaw. Hereafter referred to as *The Treasure Prompt Book*.

32. The program of *The Treasure*.

33. Sholem Aleichem *Oytsres* in *Funem Yarid*, in *Ale Verk fun Sholem Aleichem* [*Treasures* in *From The Fair* in *Complete Works of Sholem Aleichem.*] (New York: Folksfond 1923) Vol. 26 pages 32-36.

34. *The Treasure Prompt Book* 3.

35. *The Treasure Prompt Book* 3-5. The song is a variation on Avrom Volt's (Liessin) poem *Der Kremer* in *Lider Un Poemen* [*The Shopkeeper* in *Songs and Poems*] (New York: Forverts Association 1938) Vol. 1, page 224.

36. Dineson Yankev, *Zikhroynes Un Bilder* [*Memoires and Portrayals*] (Warsaw: Akhisefer) 212. The year of publication is not mentioned.

37. *The Treasure Prompt Book* 53-54.

38. Ibid. 89-90.

39. *Harishonim* [*The Pioneers*] 165.

40. The Program of *The Treasure*.

41. Interview with Berger.

42. Ibid.

43. Ibid.

44. Michael Ohad, "Habehala Lazahav" ["The Gold Rush"] in Haaretz (Tel Aviv: December 17th, 1975).

45. Interview with Berger.

46. Ibid.

47. Ibid.

48. Ibid.

49. Ibid.

50. Ibid.

51. Ibid.

52. "Hatsagat *Haotsar* al yedey Habima" [*"The Treasure* in Habima"] in Davar (Tel Aviv: November 11th, 1928).

53. Ibid.

54. Ibid.

55. Ibid.

56. Ibid.

57. N. Y., "*Haotsar*" ["*The Treasure"*] in Haaretz (Tel Aviv: December 2nd, 1928).

58. Zeitlin Hillel, "Neyn, nisht azelekhe zeynen mir, un nisht azelekhe zeynen geven unzere eltern" ["No, This Is Not How We Are, And This Is Not How Our Parents Were"] in Der Moment (Warsaw: March 21st, 1930).

59. Kazanelson Itskhok, "Der nes fun *Haotsar* in Habima" ["The miracle of *The Treasure* in Habima"] in Lodzer Togblat (Lodz March 19, 1930).

## 5. Tevye the Dairyman

1. *Dos Sholem Aleichem Bukh* 250. Like Sholem Aleichem in his correspondence I will refer to *Tevye The Dairyman* as *Tevye*.

2. Ibid. 251.

3. Shmeruk Khone, "Tevye der milkhiker - letoldoteha shel yetsira" ["Tevye The Dairyman - The Genesis of a Literary Work"] in Hasifrut (Tel Aviv: April 1978) 26, 26-39.

4. Ibid. 35.

5. Sholem Aleichem, *Tevye der Milkhiker [Tevye The Dairyman]*, adapted by I. D. Berkowitz. The manuscript is kept in Bet Shalom Aleichem in Tel Aviv.

6. Berkowitz I. D. *Tuvya hakholev* in *Kitvey Shalom Aleichem Vol 12 Makhazot [Tevye The Dairyman* in *Works Of Sholem Aleichem* Vol. 12 *Plays]* (Tel Aviv: Dvir 1950). Hereafter referred to as *Tuvya Hakholev*.

7. I interviewed Avraham Ninio at his house in Tel Aviv, December 4th 1980. Hereafter referred to as Ninio's interview.

8. *Tuvya Hakholev [Tevye The Dairyman]* 120.

9. Ibid. 162.

10. Ninio's interview.

11. The instructions for the actors are typed in Hebrew with corrections in Berkowitz's handwriting. They are kept in Bet Shalom Aleichem in Tel Aviv. Hereafter referred to as: Instructions for the Habima actors.

12. Ibid.

13. Ibid.

14. Ibid.

15. Ibid.

16. I interviewed the actor Albert Cohen at the Cameri Theater in Tel Aviv on April 4th 1980. Hereafter referred to as: Interview with Albert Cohen.

17. Ibid.

18. Interview with Rafael Klatchkin.

19. Ibid.

20. *Tuvyah Hakholev [Tevye The Dairyman]* 163.

21. Ibid. 157.

22. Ibid. 168.

23. *Dos Sholem Aleichem Bukh* [*The Sholem Aleichem Book*]117.

24. Interview with Shmuel Rodensky.

25. Interview with Hanale Händler.

26. Ibid.

27. *Hodl* in *Gants Tevye der Milkhiker* [*All Tevye The Dairyman*] 110.

28. Ibid. 195.

29. Bergson Henry, *Le Rire* [On Laughter] (Vendome: P.U.F. 1975). Hereafter referred to as: *On Laughter*

30. Interview with the actor Israel Beker in his dressing room in the Habima theater in Tel Aviv on March 12th, 1981.
    Hereafter referred to as: Interview with Israel Beker.

31. Ibid.

32. Ibid.

33. *Hodl* in *Gants Tevye der Milkhiker* [*All Tevye The Dairyman*] 115.

34. A recording is kept in the archives of the Diaspora Museum in Tel Aviv.

35. Interview with Israel Beker.

36. The Theater in Soviet Russia.

37. *25 Years of the Jewish State Theater in the Polish People's Republic* (Warsaw: Arkady 1975).

38. Frye, N. "The Myth of Spring - Comedy" in *The Anatomy of Criticism* (Princeton: Princeton University Press 1957).

39. Interview with Berger.

40. Waife Goldberg Marie, *My Father Sholem Aleichem* (New York: Schoken Books, 1971).

41. Interview with Berger.

42. Sholem Aleichem "Dos Groyse Gevins" in *Gants Tevye der Milkhiker* [*The Jackpot* in *All Tevye The Dairyman*] 15-43.
    The story was translated by Julius and Frances Butwin as *Tevye Wins a Fortune* in *The Old Country* (New York: Crown Publishers, 1946) 21-41.

43. Sholem Aleichem, *Tevye - The Eternal Optimist*. The film script is kept in Bet Shalom Aleichem in Tel Aviv. Hereafter referred to as: *Tevye - The Eternal Optimist*.

44. Ibid.

45. Ibid.

46. Ibid.

47. Ibid.

48. Ibid.

49. Ibid.

50. Ibid.

51. Sholem Aleichem, *Hava - Tevye's Daughter*. The film script is kept in Bet Shalom Aleichem in Tel Aviv. Hereafter referred to as: *Hava - Tevye's Daughter*.

52. *Dos Sholem Aleichem Bukh* [*The Sholem Aleichem Book*] 251.

53. *Hava - Tevye's Daughter.*

44. Produced in 1939 by Harry Ziskin.

45. Joseph Stein, *Tevye*. A copy of the text is kept in the Lincoln Center library for the Performing Arts in New York. The lyrics were written by Sheldon Harnick. The musical was renamed *Fiddler On The Roof*.

46. Ibid. 21.

47. Ibid. 36.

48. Joseph Stein, *Fiddler On The Roof, 1969*. A copy of the film script is kept in the film library of Tel Aviv University.

49. Vladek B.,"*Tevye der Milkhiker* in Irving Place Theater" in Forverts (New York: September 2nd 1919). Forward is the English name of the newspaper.

50. Ibid.

51. Fogelman L., "*Tevye der Milkhiker* In A Movie" ["*Tevye The Dairyman* in a Movie"] in Forverts (New York: December 25th 1939).

52. Ibid.

53. Ibid.

54. Ibid.

55. Luvrani Eliezer, "*Tuvya Hakholev* Behatsagat Habima" [*Tevye The Dairyman* in Habima]. The newspaper article is kept in the Israeli Theater Archive at Tel Aviv University.

56. Ibid.

57. Ibid.

58. Ibid.

59. R. K., "Khago shel oman" ["The Celebration of a Virtuoso"] in Devar Hapoelet (Tel Aviv: May 2nd 1950).

60. Ibid.

61. Ibid.

62. Ibid.

## 6. The Jackpot

1. *Dos Groyse Gevins - A Folksshpil In Fir Aktn [The Jackpot - A Folk Play in Four Acts]*. The manuscript complete with the variations on act three and four is kept in Bet Shalom Aleichem in Tel Aviv.

2. *The Jackpot* 19.

3. *Di Goldgreber* [*The Gold Diggers*] 555.

4. Berkowitz gave the play a new name *Amkha*. Literally "Your people"."Amkha" is a folksy designation for a Jewish person. The play is included in *Komediot* in *Kitvey Shalom Aleichem*, Vol. 11 [*Comedies* in *Works of Sholem Aleichem* Vol. 11] (Tel Aviv: Dvir 1950) 125-223. Hereafter referred to as *Amkha*.

5. Ibid. 128-129

6. Ibid. 144.

7. *The Jackpot* 19.

8. *Amkha* [*Your People*] 125.

9. Ibid. 205-206.

10. *The Jackpot* 39.

11. *Amkha* [*Your People*] 122.

12. *The Jackpot* 19.

13. *Amkha* [*Your People*] 125.

14. *The Jackpot* 19. We translated Sholem Aleichem's "Before the war" as "Before the first world war".

15. Litvakov M., *Finf Yor Melukhisher Yidisher Kamer Teater [Five Years of the Jewish State Chamber Theater]* (Moscow: "Shul Un Bukh" 1924). Hereafter referred to as *Finf Yor Melukhisher Yidisher Kamer Teater*.

16. Dobrushin Y., *Binyomin Zuskin* (Moscow: Der Emes 1939) 15. Hereafter referred to as *Binyomin Zuskin*.

17. *Finf Yor Melukhisher Yidisher Kamer Teater* [*Five Years of the Jewish State Chamber Theater*] 75.

18. Ibid. 75.

19. Ibid. 75-76.

20. Sachs Arieh, *Shkiat Halets* [*The Waning of the Fool*] (Tel Aviv: Sifriyat Hapoalim 1978).

21. *Das Moskauer Jüdische Akademische Theater* [*The Moscow Jewish Academic Theater*](Berlin: Die Schmiede 1928). Hereafter referred to as: Das Moskau Jüdische Akademische Theater.

22. *Binyomin Zuskin* 15.

23. Artaud Antonin, *Le Théâtre Et Son Double* [*The Theater and its Double*] (Saint Amand: 1970).

24. *Binyomin zuskin* 16.

25. Lubomirsky Yeshua, *Af Di Lebnsvegn* [*On Life's Roads*] (Moscow: Sovetsky Pisatel 1976)

26. Ibid. 155.

27. Barna Yon, *The Complete Films Of Eisenstein* (New York: E. P. Dutton & Co. Inc. 1974) 24.

28. Ibid. 70.

29. Duchartre Pierre Louis, *La Comédie Italienne* [*The Italian Comedy*] (Paris: Librairie De France 1925).

30. Khashin A., "Der sheferisher veg funem moskver yidishn melukhe teater" in *Tsen Yor Artef* ["The Creative Way of the Moscow Yiddish State Theater" in *Ten Years of the Artef*] (New York: 1937) page 84. Hereafter referred to as: Khashin's article.

31. Ibid. 79-80.

32. Ibid. 80.

33. The recording is kept in the Diaspora Museum in Tel Aviv.

34. *Finf Yor Melukhisher Yidisher Kamer Teater* [ *Five Years of the Jewish State Chamber Theater]* 74.

35. Shayn Yosef, *Arum Moskver Yidishn Teater* [*Around the Moscow Yiddish Theater*] (Paris: Les Editions Polyglottes 1964) 54.

36. Khashin's article 81.

37. *Finf Yor Melukhisher Yidisher Kamer Teater* [*Five Years of the Jewish State Chamber Theater*] 78.

38. Sartre Jean Paul, *Anti-Semite and Jew* Trans. by J. Becker *(New York: Schocken 1965).*

39. Joseph Roth in the preface to the album *Das Moskauer Jüdische Akademische Theater* [*The Moscow Jewish Academic Theater*].

40. Dovid Sfard wrote about Yankev Rotboym in his book *Shtudyes un Skitsn* [*Studies and Sketches*] (Warsaw: Farlag Yidish Bukh: 1955) 86-195.

Rotboym himself wrote an article: "My Work with the Jewish State Theater in the Years 1949-1974" in *25 Years Of The Jewish State Theater In The Polish People's Republic* 20-26.

41. *Dos Groyse Gevins* [*The Jackpot*] - the stage adaptation by Yankev Rotboym for the production in The Polish Jewish State Theater, (Warsaw 1973) 30-32. Hereafter referred to as: Rotboym's *Dos Groyse Gevins.*

42. Interview with Yankev Rotboym at his home in Wroclaw, in April 1979. Hereafter referred to as: Interview with Rotboym.

43. Interview with Rotboym.

44. *Dos Sholem Aleichem Bukh* [*The Sholem Aleichem Book*].

45. Interview with Rotboym.

46. Rotboym's *Dos Groyse Gevins* [*The Jackpot*]89.

47. Ionesco Eugene, *Notes Et Contre Notes* [*Notes and Counter Notes*] (Saint Amand: Gallimard 1975) 63.

48. The text is Sholem Aleichem's *Dos Gryose Gevins* [*The Jackpot*] in the 1917 Folksfond edition with hand written remarks by Rotboym. Page 40. The book is kept in Rotboym's archive in Wroclaw. Hereafter referred to as: Rotboym's first adaptation.

49. *On Laughter.*

50. Interview with Rotboym.

51. *The Jackpot* 44.

52. Rotboym's first adaptation.

53. *Funem Yarid* [*From the Fair*]11-12.

54. Interview with Rotboym.

55. Ibid.

56. Rotbym showed me pictures from his and Granovsky's production in our interview at his home archive in Wroclaw. Pictures in print from the Granovsky and Rotboym productions can be found respectively in *Das Moskauer Jüdische Akademische Teater* [*The Moscow Jewish Academic Theater*] and in *25 Years Of The Jewish State Theater In The Polish People's Republic*.

57. Interview with Rotboym.

58. Ibid.

59. Ibid.

60. Ibid.

61. Ibid.

62. Ibid.

63. Ibid.

64. Ibid.

65. Ibid.

66. Ibid.

67. Ibid.

68. Dos Groyse Gevins [*The Jackpot*]17.

69. Interview with Rotboym.

70. Interview with Peter Frei at his home in Ramat Aviv on March 14th 1978.

71. Interview with Rotboym.

72. Ibid.

73. Ibid.

74. Fogelman l., "Sholem Aleichem's *Dos Groyse Gevins* in der Folksbine" ["Sholem Aleichem's *The Jackpot* in the Folksbine"] in Forverts (New York: February 2nd 1945).

75. Ibid.

76. Ginzberg D., "A frabenreikher spektakl, ober..." ["A colorful show, but"...] in Folksshtime (Warsaw: May 5th, 1964).

77. Ibid.

78. Ibid.

79. Ibid.

80. Ulrich Seelman - Eggbert, "Zweites Gastspiel des Warschauer Jüdischen Theaters in Basel - Errinerung an vergangene Zeiten" ["Second Performance of the Warsaw Jewish Theater in Basel -Memories about bygone Times"] in Basler National Zeitung (Basel: May 5th 1976).

81. Manger Itsik, *Lid Un Balade* [*Song and Ballad*] (Tel Aviv: Itsik Manger Komitet & Letste Nayes) 369. Note: The year of publication is not mentioned.

## 7. Epilogue

1. *Meyerhold on Theater*, Translated and edited by E. Braun (Chatham: Methuen: 1969) 49-58.

2. Interview with Bunim.

# Selected Bibliography of the Plays

The bulk of Sholem Aleichem's dramatic work is compiled in three volumes of *Ale Verk fun Sholem Aleicehem* [*Complete works of Sholem Aleichem*] (New York: Folksfond:1923).

Volume 4 *Dramatishe Shriftn* [Dramatic Works] includes 4 short plays and one full length comedy: *The Jackpot*.

| | |
|---|---|
| *Der get* [*The Divorce*] | 7-40 |
| *Tsezeyt un tseshpreyt* [*Scattered and Dispersed*] | 41-98 |
| *A dokter* [*A Doctor*] | 117-150 |
| *Dos Groyse Gevins* [*The Jackpot*] | 151-256 |

Volume 24. *Komedyes* [*Comedies*] includes ten one-acts:

| | |
|---|---|
| *Di Asife* [*The Convention*] | 7-28 |
| *YOKENHOZ* | 29-134 |
| *Mazel Tov* | 135-168 |
| *Farbitn di Yotsres* [*Trading places*] | 169-198 |
| *Agentn* [*Agents*] | 197-218 |
| *Keynig Pik* [*King Pique*] | 219-236 |
| *Shrage* | 237-263 |
| *Oylem Habe* [*Heaven*] | 263-280 |
| *Mister Boym in Kloset* [*Mister Boym in the Closet*] | 281-290 |
| *Intsveyen a zeks un zekhtsig* [*The Two Combined 66*] | 291-303 |

Volume 25 *Fun Tsvey Veltn* [*From Two Worlds*] includes two plays.

| | |
|---|---|
| *Shver tsu zayn a Yid* [*It's hard to be a Jew*] | *8-164* |
| *Tevye der milkhiker* [*Tevye The Dairyman*] | 165-235 |

The plays were reprinted unchanged in a later Folksfond edition in 1927 and in the Morgn Frayhayt edition in 1937. The only difference is in the order of the volumes. *Komedyes, Fun Tsvey Veltn*, and *Dramatishe Shriftn* are respectively volumes 5, 6, and 20. The pagination remained the same.

*Di Goldgreber* [*The Gold diggers*] which is the second title for *The Treasure*] was not included in *Ale Verk fun Sholem Aleichem* [*complete works of Sholem Aleichem*] although it is one of his best plays. The play was published in <u>Di Zukunft</u> (New York: 1927, October, November, December issues) 555-568, 618-623, 682-687.

*Stempenyu* was never published. The novel that served for the dramatic adaptaion was translated by H. Berman (London: Methuen and Co., 1913).

*Dovid Ben Dovid* [*David Son Of David*] was published in Di Goldene Keyt 34 (Tel Aviv:1959) 18-47.

## Plays in English Translation

*Heaven [Oylem Habe)]* in *Sholem Aleichem Panorama*, ed. M. W. Grafstein (Jewish Observer: London-Ontario 1948) 263-280.

*It's Hard to Be A Jew [Shver tsu zayn a yid)]*, Ibid. 7-164.

*The Jackpot*, [(*Dos Groyse Gevins*)] translated by Kobi Weitzner and Barnett Zumoff (New York: The Workmen's Circle Education Department: 1989).

*She Must Marry A Doctor* [*A Dokter*] in *Six plays from the Yiddish Theater*, ed. Isaac Goldberg (Boston: Luce 1913) 99-115.

## Plays in Hebrew Translation

I. D. Berkowitz translated his Yiddish adaptations of *Tevye* and *It's Hard To Be A Jew*. He wrote both adaptations for Maurice Schwartz's Art Theater [Kunst Teater] in New York. Berkowitz translated one one-act *Mentshn* [*Domestics*]. The three plays are included in *Kitvey Shalom Aleichem* [*Works of Sholem Aleichem*]. They had numerous reprints. The edition used in this book is that of 1950. Vol. 12 entitled *Makhazot* [*Plays*] 8-94, 95-174, 174-202. Berkowitz also made Hebrew adaptations of three Sholem Aleichem comedies: *The Jackpot*, *The Treasure* and *Mazel Tov*. The three comedies are included in *Kitvey Shalom Aleichem* [*Works of Sholem Aleichem*] Vol 11 entitled *Komediot* [*Comedies*] (Tel Aviv: Dvir 1950) 7-122, 123-223, 224-255.

Arieh Aharoni, the most recent Sholem Aleichem translator, failed in his attempt to present Sholem Aleichem to the Israeli reader in a contemporary Hebrew as opposed to the flowery Hebrew Style of I.D. Berkowitz. With all the reservation one might have about Berkowitz's style and the liberties he took with the texts, his are still the best versions available of Sholem Aleichem plays in Hebrew.

Aharoni translated the bulk of Sholem Aleichem dramatic work. He covered volumes 4, 24, and 25 of *Ale Verk* complete with *Di Goldgreber* [*The Gold Diggers*] and compiled them in one volume *Makhazot Umaarkhonim* [*Plays and One Act Plays*]. (Tel Aviv: Sifriyat Hopoalim 1988). The translated plays are:

| | |
|---|---|
| *Haget* [*The Divorce*] | 13-38 |
| *Mefuzarim umefuradim* [*Scattered and dispersed*] | 39-90 |
| *Doktor* [*Doctor*] | 91-106 |
| *Meshartim* [*Domestics*] | 107-134 |
| *Hazkhiya Hagdoala* [*The Jackpot*] | 135-218 |
| *Khofrey Hazahav* [*The Gold Diggers*] | 219-318 |
| *Tuvya Hakhalban* [*Tevye the Milkman*] | 319-382 |
| *Haasefa* [*The Convention*] | 383-402 |
| YOKENHOZ | 403-490 |
| *Mazal Tov* [*Mazel Tov*] | 491-520 |
| *Hekhlifu et Hayotsrot* [*Trading Places*] | 521-544 |
| *Agentim* [*Agents*] | 545-564 |
| *Melekh Pik* [*King Pique*] | 565-578 |
| *Shraga* | 579-600 |
| *Olam Haba* [*Heaven*] | 601-616 |
| *Mister Boym Baaron* [*Mister Boym in the Closet*] | 617-624 |
| *Shishim veshesh Bishnayim* [*The Two Combined 66*] | 625-635 |

Aharoni's translation of "Agentn" ["Agents"] as "Agentim" is incomprehensible to native Hebrew speakers who would use the word "sokhnim".

## Additional Sources

Uriel Weinreich wrote a selected bibliography on Sholem Aleichem in
   *The Field Of Yiddish - Studies in Yiddish Language Folklore and
   Literature*. (New York: Linguistic Circle of New York 1954) 278-291.
The bibliography contains information about Sholem Aleichem plays in
   Yiddish and in translation. To my knowledge, except my translation
   of *The Jackpot* no further Sholem Aleichem plays were published in
   English since the publication of Uriel Weinreich's Sholem Aleichem
   bibliography.

Zalmen Zylbercweig gives a survey of Sholem Aleichem plays in volume
   4 of his *Lexikon fun Yidishn Teater [Lexicon of Yiddish Theater]*
   (New York: Hebrew Union Actors of America, Farlag Elisheva 1963).
   3309-3578. Zylbercweig gives a bibliography of the plays and their
   press reviews.

Khone Shmeruk's *Shalom Aleichem - Madrich Lekhayav Uleyetsirato
   [Sholem Aleichem - A Guide to his Life and Work]* (Tel Aviv:
   Publications of The Porter Institute for Poetics and Semiotics 1980)
   contains a chapter "*Hadramot*" ["*The Dramas*"] about Sholem
   Aleichem plays. The chapter (69-75) gives a chronology of Sholem
   Aleichem's plays.
According to Shmeruk Sholem Aleichem's Plays written before *Tseseyt
   un tseshpreyt [Scattered and Dispersed]* were published in a
   scientific edition: *Dramatishe Shriftn [Dramatic Works]* with
   introduction and commentaries by N. Oyslender, In Kharkov and
   Kiev in 1932. This is volume 19 of the unfinished Soviet *Gesamelte
   Verk [Complete Works]*. The consecutive volumes were not published.
   Thus the Soviet version of *Ale Verk* [Complete Works] does not
   contain any of Sholem Aleichem major plays.

## Selected Bibliography of Sholem Aleichem Works in English

*Adventures of Menachem-Mendel*, Trans. by Tamara Kahana (New York: Putnam's sons, 1969. Reprinted in New York: Paper Back Library, 1970).

*From the Fair*, Trans. by Curt Leviant (New York: Viking Penguin Inc. 1985).

*Holiday Tales of Sholem Aleichem*, Trans. by Aliza Shevrin (New York: Charles Scribner's Sons, 1979).

*Inside Kasrilivke*, Trans. by Isidore Goldstick (New York: Shocken Books, 1965. Reprinted in New York: Schoken Paperback, 1968).

*Jewish Children*, Trans. by Hannah Berman (New York: Alfred Knopf, 1926. Reprinted in New York: Bloch Publishing Co., 1937).

*Old Country Tales*, Trans. by Curt Leviant (New York: G. P. Putnam's Sons, 1966).

*Selected Stories of Sholom Aleichem*, Introduction by Alfred Kazin, Trans. by Isaac Rosenfeld, Shlomo Katz, Julius and Frances Butwin (New York: Modern Library, 1956).

*Stempenyu, Trans. by H. Berman (London: Methuen & Co. 1913).*

*Stories and Satires*, Trans. by Curt Leviant. (New York: Thomas Yoseloff, 1959. Reprinted in London: Collier Books, 1970).

*Tevye's Daughters*, Trans. by Frances Butwin (New York: Crown Publishers, 1949).

*The Adventures of Motl: The Cantor's son*, Trans. by Tamara Kahana (New York: Abelard Shuman, 1961).

*The Best of Sholem Aleichem,* Edited by Irving Howe and Ruth R. Wisse (Washington: New Republic Books, 1979).

*The Bewitched Tailor*, Trans. by Bernard Isaacs (Moscow: Foreign Languages Publishing House).

*The Bloody Hoax*, Trans. by Aliza Shevrin (Bloomington: Indiana University Press, 1991).

*The Great Fair*, Trans. by Tamara Kahana (New York: Noonday Press, 1955. Reprinted in New York: Noonday Paperback, 1958).

*The Old Country*, Trans. by Julius and Frances Butwin (New York: Crown Publishers, 1946).

*Some Laughter some Tears*, Trans. by Curt Leviant (New York: Paperback Library 1969).

*The Tevye Stories and Others*, Trans. by Julius and Frances Butwin (New York: Pocket Books, 1965).

*The World of Sholem Aleichem*, Trans. by Maurice Samuel (Alfred A. Knopf, 1943).

*Treasury of Yiddish Stories*, Edited by Irving Howe and Eliezer Greenberg (Viking Press, 1953).

*Wandering Stars*, Trans. by Frances Butwin (New York: Crown Publishers, 1952).

*Why Do the Jews Need a Land of Their Own?*, Trans. by Joseph Leftwich and Mordecai S. Chertoff (Tel Aviv: Bet Shalom Aleichem, 1984).

# Index

**A**

Adler, Jacob   5
Aristotle   9
Artaud, Antonin   119 - 120

**B**

Berger, Juliusz   58, 64 - 70, 92 - 95, 152
Bergson, Henri   70, 89, 135
Bertonov, Yehoshua   67, 71, 108
Brecht, Bertold   35, 51, 126, 149
Broderson, Moyshe   130, 133
Bunim, Shmuel   21 - 25, 28 - 35, 37 - 38, 63, 152
Burstein Family   21
Buzgan, Chewel   57 - 60, 62 - 64, 66, 92 - 93, 95

**C**

Chaplin, Charlie   122, 135
Chemerinsky, Baruch   50, 81, 85, 108
Cohen, Albert   83 - 84, 86, 88
*Comedia dell'arte*   24 - 25, 50 - 51, 56, 122 - 123

**D**

*Di Vilner Trupe*, see *Vilna Troupe*   129, 134
*Di Yidishe Folksbibliotek*, see *Jewish Folk Library*   2, 43 - 44
Dicky, Alexander   32, 50 - 56, 62, 66, 71 - 72, 150 - 152
Dineson, Yankev   61
Dobrushin, Y.   89 - 90, 116 - 117, 125 - 126
*Dybbuk, The (Anski)*   18, 55, 72, 129

## E
Eisenstein, Sergey, 51

## F
Fogelman 106 - 107
Folksbine 21, 31 - 32, 145 - 147
Frei, Peter 144 - 145
*Frivolity and Hypocrisy*, (Wolfson) 13
*From the Fair* (Sholem Aleichem) 1, 7, 60
Frye, Northrop 92
*Funem Yarid*, see *From the Fair* 1, 7, 60

## G
Galsworthy, John 115
Goldfaden, Avrom 16, 35 - 36, 61 - 62, 68
Granovsky, Alexander 10 - 11, 51, 59, 68, 91, 102, 115 - 130, 132 - 134, 137 - 140, 144, 146 - 147, 149, 151 - 152

## H
Habima 8, 21, 32, 34, 48, 50, 52, 55 - 56, 66 - 67, 70 - 73, 79 - 81, 85 - 88, 107 - 109, 151
Händler, Hanale 54, 66, 87 - 88
*Haskala* 16, 49

## I
*In the Synagogue Anteroom* (Peretz) 44
Ionesco, Eugene 134
Italian comedy 122 - 123

## J
Jewish State Chamber Theater *see* Moscow Jewish State Theater
Jewish Folk Library, The (Sholem Aleichem) 2 - 3, 12, 43 - 44

## K
Kazanelson, Itskhok 72
Kessler, David 42, 63

Khashin, A.   124 - 125
Klatchkin, Rafael   35, 48, 50, 55 - 56, 83 - 84, 88
*Klezmer*   21, 23, 25, 27 - 28, 30, 34
Kon, Henoch   130, 133

**L**
Litvakov, Moyshe   116 - 117, 127
Luckacz, F.L.   18

**M**
Manger, Itsik   21, 24, 149
Markish, Peretz   109
Mendele Moykher Sforim   2, 12, 20, 72
Meyerhold, Vsevolod   50, 122, 147, 150 - 152
Mikhoels Shloyme   89 - 91, 109 - 110
Moscow Jewish State Theater   89, 91, 109, 115, 123, 125, 129

**N**
Niger, Shmuel   20, 43
Ninio, Avraham   80 - 81, 84

**O**
Oyslender, N.   89 - 90, 125 - 126

**P**
Peretz, Yitskhok Leyb   2, 44 - 45, 109, 124
Pinsky, Dovid   75 - 76, 99
*Purimshpil*   25 - 28, 37

**R**
Reinhardt, Max   51
Rodensky, Shmuel   52, 86
Rotboym, Yankev   11, 129 - 149, 152
Roth, Joseph   128
Rumshinsky, Yosef   19

## S

Sartre, Jean Paul  128
Schneider, Beno  59
Schwartz, Maurice  7, 9, 32 - 33, 75, 79, 99 - 102, 106 - 108, 110, 125, 152
*Selling of Joseph, The*  26, 61
Shabtay, Yaacov  30 - 31, 34
Sheikevitch, Nokhem Meir  12
Shmeruk, Khone  76 - 78
*shund*  12 - 15, 17, 20 - 21, 34, 36, 47, 72, 115
shomer  see Sheikevitch 12
Stanislavsky, Constantin  51 - 52, 123, 140
Stein, Joseph  102 - 105
Szwejlich, Moyshe  57 - 59

## T

Thomashefsky, Boris  5, 14 - 15, 19 - 20, 36, 42
Topol, Haim  9, 104

## V

Vakhtangov, Yevgeny  50, 55, 72
Vilna Troupe  125, 129, 134, 145, 149

## W

Wolfson, Aaron  13

## Y

YIVO  15

## Z

Zeitlin, Hilel  71 - 72
Zuskin, Binyomin  116, 120
Zylbercweig, Zalem  10